POETRY now

Perception Of Place

Edited by

Andrew Head

First published in Great Britain in 1998 by
POETRY NOW
1-2 Wainman Road, Woodston,
Peterborough, PE2 7BU
Telephone (01733) 230746
Fax (01733) 230751

HB ISBN 1 86188 614 4
SB ISBN 1 86188 609 8

FOREWORD

Although we are a nation of poetry writers we are accused of not reading poetry and not buying poetry books: after many years of listening to the incessant gripes of poetry publishers, I can only assume that the books they publish, in general, are books that most people do not want to read.

Poetry should not be obscure, introverted, and as cryptic as a crossword puzzle: it is the poet's duty to reach out and embrace the world.

The world owes the poet nothing and we should not be expected to dig and delve into a rambling discourse searching for some inner meaning.

The reason we write poetry (and almost all of us do) is because we want to communicate: an ideal; an idea; or a specific feeling. Poetry is as essential in communication, as a letter; a radio; a telephone, and the main criteria for selecting the poems in this anthology is very simple: they communicate.

Different people have different perceptions of place. They have all been brought together in this book to give the reader a rough guide to life.

There is a wide variety of poems within the collection. They vary from tales of exotic countries to life in general.

The poems are written by the unknown poets of today. They deal with the emotions and stresses of different places they have been within their lives.

We are able to get a true insight into people's 'perception of place'.

Contents

Never To-Be-Forgotten	Dorothy Thompson	1
My Heart's Retreat	Helen Shenton	2
Sweetshop	Rita Bull	3
Song Of The Linnet	Gill Cordy	4
A Frosty Domain	Natalie Russell	5
Caerphilly Castle	Joan Kennedy	6
The Old Grey Stone Walls	Linda Tosney	7
Anticipation	June Hilliar	8
Whitstable Market	Patricia Holman	9
Shaldon	Gillian S Roberts	10
Fawkland Square	R P Avery	11
Music On The Train	John Brooks	12
The Beach	Julie Titchener	13
In Hospital	Pauline Friend	14
Bright Scarf	S Greenhalgh	15
Shoreline	Alison Glithro	16
Upon The Hillside	Nadia Darwish	17
Turn Tail	Valerie Brown	18
Summer Storm	Sylvia Spence	19
Slab Square C 1970	Gary Roe	20
Lady Of The Lake (Llyn Ogwen)	Norman Royal	21
Night Delights	Anna Walker	22
So Green Is My Valley	Robert Gerald	23
The Underground	David R Williams	24
The Shopping Centre	Elizabeth Ross	25
Sense Of Place	Amanda Louise Thompson	26
Dust Mite	Jim Powell Hill	27
Broadstairs Bay	Dave Lunn	28
I sensed The Crafts Of Yesteryear	Wenn-The-Penn	29
Single Beauty	Patricia Madden	30
Postnatal Separation	Shirley Frost	31
A Better Place	Joy Benford	32

The School	Dorothy Whitehall	33
Puesta Del Sol	David Atkinson	34
Heaven Is In The Northern Hills	Knutsson	35
The Shore	Samantha Douglas	36
Fire	Teresa Booth	37
The Lighthouse	Martin Edmonds	38
Sea Signs	C Shadwell	39
Hidden Valley	P M Lightfoot	40
Cliffs Of County Clare	H Val Forsfall	41
Tall-Ships	Maisie Roberts	42
The Ring Of Kerry	Celia Law	43
Changing Scenes	Betty M Varley	44
Changes	Christine Kelly	45
Palace Style	Tina Nyamebah Edwards	46
Island	Pat Cooper	47
Reality	A J Marshall	48
The Shallows	Jose Lacey	49
The Laburnum Tree	Jennifer Bailey	50
Scunthorpe	Stan Downing	51
Summer Season	V Brickley	52
A Walk By The Canal	Carol Barrett	53
The Abbey Ruins	Barbara Fitzgerald	54
Happy Days	Win	55
Edge Of The Rain	S Peter Robson	56
The Ideal End	Christine Thomas	57
A Special Lure	Danielle Linton	58
Rottingdean 1997	Dennis Jenkinson	59
The Cherry Orchard	Poppy Ashfield	60
Hill Of Gold	Susan Green	61
Istanbul May 1997	Gill Kipps	62
I Wandered Lonely As A Child	Mary Jayne Evans	63
Dreamland. Bus 7. Stand E	Francis B Rylance	64
The Geriatric Ward	Patricia Jamieson	65
Brighton Wakes Up	Matthew W Jones	66

Mind Travels	Jayne Jenkins	67
Flesh Shop	Stephen Bone	68
Take A Look Around	Barbara D Grindy	69
Winter's Wings	Deborah Hickson	70
My Home	D M Haworth	71
The Need	Betty Dobson	72
The Somerset Levels	Carol Exten-Wright	73
Burial Of A Beggar Man	Alex Branthwaite	74
La Tour Jeanne D'Arc, Rouen	Betty Everson	75
Ring Of Stones	Carole Anne Johnson	76
Cattle Market	Annemarie Poole	77
A Vista Of White	Pamela Sears	78
Thoughts On A Garden	Edwin Heath	79
My Shangri-La	Patricia Edwards	80
Jacaranda	S McDermott	81
Rickmansworth Memory	G Winwright	82
Prague	John A Davis	83
Romanian Impressions	Joanna Watson	84
Outpatients	J Brookes	85
Our Library	S F Barrett	86
The Churchyard	Bruce Wiseman	87
Millersdale	Joyce Neville	88
Hampshire Water	Denis M Pentlow	89
Dorset	E Chaffey	90
The Incident	J Fish	91
A Kestrel For A Knave Indeed	J W Gummerson	92
Springtime	Susan A Peach	93
St Mary's Lighthouse	Pat Berkshire	94
The Dying Room	Julie Macleod	95
El Agheila -1943	Rannoch Melville Russell	96
An Endless Love	Vera Clarke	97
Mirth Angel	Jean Paisley	98
Seascape	CL	100
On Water Leaving Great Shunner Fell	David Higgins	101

Virunga National Park, Ziare	K F Adamson	102
Bad Memories	David Rhine	103
Look, Stranger!	Doreen McPherson	104
Up-River	Alan Cole	105
Treescape In Provence: Perpetuum Mobile	Anne Sanderson	106
Sense Of Place	George Jeffery	107
A Wessex Hill	J C Turner	108
The Old House	C Giles	109
The Joys Within My Garden	Yvonne Watkin-Rees	110
Born By The Wash	Fleur Lusher	111
Precious Time	Ivan George Barber	112
Cornwall	J Guy	113
A View	Mike Naylor	114
My Bath	Tina Smith	115
Evening At St Brelade's Bay	Rosaline Pilley	116
The Urban Knight	Tim Warren	117
The Mountain	Susie Barker	118
Colours In Tunisia	Charmian Goldwyn	120
Northern Delights	Iain Barr	121
I Knew That You Were There	Antoni Strich	122
Lecture Of Roses And Hearths	Alex Guthrie	124
Ghost Town	Patricia Widdowson	125
Caerphilly Mountain	Eileen Brown	126
Snake	Hamish Lee	127
Scotland	V G Walker	128
Deserted	Gareth Lewis-Jones	129
The Ghost City	Dianne J Shorthouse	130
Crete	Emma Fordham	131
Panacea For Sleeplessness	Felicity M Bradley	132
My Garden	Olive Eves	133
A Field Asleep	Sean Rooney	134
Kasbah	Alison Dugmore	135
Sense Of Place	Emma Cottell	136
My Meadow	Evelyn Ingram	137

Sweet Sorrow	Andrea Noelle Vaughan	138
A Shopping Centre	Lynda Hughes	139
Sunset	A S McKay	140
Two Faces Of Goa	Brenda H Bradbury	141
California Again	Pam Redmond	142
Walking Back To Durdle-Door	Gladys Llewellyn	143
Bussing It	Bernadette Morris	144
Untitled	Iain A Murray	146
Waterscape	Mandy Pannett	147
The Scent Of The Lilies	Sandra Lewis	148
Cardiff Bay	Ray Lewis	149
Newark-On-Trent	D Mitchell	150
Villages Of Mystery	Roger Hodges	151
At Watergate Bay	Irene Snatt	152
Rest By The Riverside	Ruby Ling	153
Train From London	Helen Pisarska	154
On Call	Jacquie Dimmer	155
Sea Ghosts	W E Hobson	156
Sunset In Provence	Evelyn Westwood	157
Paws For Thought	Pauline A Wicks	158
Winter Warmth	Wendy Brennan	159
My Garden	Carol Deakin	160
Escaping	Deborah Carol Hughes	161
On Leaving Ilfracombe One Sunday In June '78 . . .	Irene G Corbett	162
Clouds	Sheila Duguid	163
Timeless	Amanda-Lea Manning	164
Thankfully	T Stevenson	166
Gloucestershire Harvest	Gary Bills	167
Past-Present	Nicolette E Jones	168
An Enchanted Island	G M Neary	169
But On An Impulse	Martin Summers	170
The Beach	Lisa Horner	171
At Sails Point	L C Hawke	172
The Harebell	Maureen Cropley	174

Never-To-Be-Forgotten

Never-to-be-forgotten ethereal sound
In surreal surroundings -
A Parisian cemetery!

Sightseeing weariness caused us
To wander away from the crowds,
So we sat, pondering the strange houses
In this village of the dead -
Bizarre buildings with mysterious
Interiors that sheltered - nobody!
Godforsaken it seemed in spite of
The eulogies and glowing phrases.

Above us, the sky was dark with clouds
Lying across the blue, like so many shrouds
To hide the sun. Then, suddenly,
A shaft of light illuminated all about
And it was warm. Like damp confetti
On our heads a gentle drizzle sprinkled us.

A transformation then began beneath the
Rainbow arching there, and, in that instant,
Piercing through the air we heard
A silver note float clean and pure
And then descend into a moan -
The aching heart, the seared soul
Of someone's tenor saxophone.

Silence now was everywhere:
Spellbound we listened to that lonely sound;
Never-to-be-forgotten memory, one day
In a Parisian cemetery.

Dorothy Thompson

My Heart's Retreat

The land is calling,
The land is calling.
Throughout this dark night.
Open the door!
Let me see
The thunder and lightning so late!

Flash! Crash!
Will it split the tree in two?
It almost touched the ground that time!
Wild summer storm in my heart's retreat.

Run around the hilltop
The morning sun has cleared the storm.
Up and down, round and round,
Mounds and depths
But keep up with the chase!

Faster and faster! They cannot catch me!
I'm young and nimble
And I'm far too happy.
My brother, myself and our old dear friend.

Helen Shenton

Sweetshop

When I was young, say nine or ten
everything was nicer then,
with sixpence in my hand I'd stop
to gaze into my favourite shop,
such a problem what to pick
acid drops or liquorice stick
round gob-stoppers, toffee dab
home-made fudge set in a slab
or sherbet lemons nice and sharp
pineapple chunks or apple tarts,
to see them all I'd stand tiptoe
that little girl of long ago,
and then with sixpence wisely spent
pockets bulging home I went.
The shop has gone now, in its place,
a dentist's surgery fills the space.

Rita Bull

Song Of The Linnet

Oh, sweet linnet,
high in my tree,
why are you singing
so sweetly to me?

One for laughter
and two for mirth,
the ways of cheering
this lovely old earth.

Three for fragrance,
tall trees and lawn,
four for golden reds
colouring the dawn.

Five for freshness
of each new day,
six for the colour
brightening the grey.

Seven for joy,
birds on the wing,
eight for the rainbow,
that makes my heart sing.

Nine for wonder
of stars above
and dreaming deeply
of this life and love.

Ten for sorrow
at this, the end
of the pretty song
of my feathered friend.

Gill Cordy

A Frosty Domain

I'll come for you
As I sweep.
I'll reap your life in
As you sleep
Alone in your bed
Little flower
'Cause I am the tune
Of the quiet killer.

Cheerful tree, all
Leaves in bloom,
I am your calendar and
I'll come for you as soon
As I can, wait,
Taste my cold
I'll cover you in tears
Of summers of old.

I'll carpet the grass
With crystal bells
You will not know
Till I've covered the fells
No-one knows me yet
I live a short time -
I smell of my victim's fragrance
But I see no crime.

Natalie Russell

CAERPHILLY CASTLE

Summer pours down like thick honey,
warming groups of whispering visitors,
here they flock by the coach load,
taking a swift peek into history.
How icy the air of ages past,
and silent behind stout, stone walls,
smell the reek of banquets gone,
and the blood and guts of war
are eaten into the brave walls,
arrow slits keep out the sun,
while dungeons keep silent screams
that can only be heard in the mind.
Here is graffiti of a more recent past . . .
'Bron luvs Dai'
'Cardiff City rules OK'
'English go home',
defiling tormented walls
where once days were painfully chipped away . . .
covered now by active lichen.
Seen from the shaky tower
that crumbles more at every touch,
the moat is bright, murky mysterious,
green-breasted swans
bending noble heads in disdain.
From the moat reaches a grassy twmp,
and the dropped drawbridge
to a circle of enclosing walls
that protects the castle within.
Here live whispers that echo down the years,
a sudden laugh is muffled
by a rush of reverence
to the ghosts
of Caerphilly Castle.

Joan Kennedy

The Old Grey Stone Walls

From the old, grey stone walls
The ancient ones call
For us to come and listen
As to how they became
Trapped in their prison.

The wise men of old
Revered a plinth of stone.
They believed that it held
Great powers of wealth
So we worshipped it ourselves.

We built stone circles
With an altar in the middle
Where we offered sacrifices.
Sometimes it was the living,
Will we ever be forgiven?

What we did not comprehend
Was the stones' sole intent
Until it was too late
The hard cold stone
Had taken us for its own

So when you are walking
Across the wild open moors
And you hear a moanful wailing
Do not be frightened or alarmed
It's only the old grey stone walls.

Linda Tosney

ANTICIPATION

The dentist's waiting room
Is a place of fear.
Not knowing quite
What awaits you there.
Sitting staring
At the floor,
Magazines piled up
By the door.
Muffled noises
Sound like drills,
The very thought
Makes you feel ill.
After a while
You hear your name.
You'd do a runner
If you weren't in pain.
Come inside and
Into the chair.
Open wide,
Ah we're nearly there.
A rotten tooth
It will soon be out,
Oh blessed relief
As you give a shout.
Well it wasn't as bad
As you thought it would be,
It's the waiting that hurts,
But at last you feel free.

June Hilliar

Whitstable Market

Thursday again,
what bustle, what choice.
Well polished fruit, clean vegetables
some quite strange.
Curtains, toys, tools for sale.
Clothes, sweets, videos and loud 60's music.

Also, hidden amongst the professionals
is the 'Cat Lady' with her Aladdin's cave.
Curlers and costumes,
flowers and fancy goods
bric-a-brac and bags
shoes and soft toys.

However tired this little lady must be
she always has a smile and a joke.
Always on the 'go', battling with the elements
searching for a lost feline
or taking in a stray.

Where would a market be
without these good souls who toil for others
whose purpose seems to be
to devote their energies in rescuing,
resuscitating, sustaining those animals
less fortunate than us
but oh! so much more rewarding than us.

Patricia Holman

SHALDON

Shaldon is a small village in Devon.
It is my little slice of heaven.
Nestling at the mouth of the River Teign.
For hundreds of years more or less the same.
Just like stepping back in time,
A gentler pace and peace of mind.

A little thatched cottage - roses round the door,
Who could ask for anything more.
A river beach just down the road,
Viewed from the window a sight to behold.
The ferry crosses this busy river,
To and fro hither and thither.

A trip to Teignmouth you can take,
If a shopping spree you wish to make.
Shaldon has some good shops too,
And all the shopping there you can do.
The well-known landmark of the Ness,
Stays in the heart with tenderness.

Smugglers tunnel through to the beach,
The only way it can be reached,
Unless at low tide you climb round the rocks.
When the tide is high this way it blocks.
If in Shaldon, wave goodbye to time,
To watch the clock is such a crime.

When walking you can meet a friend,
As round the narrow roads you wend.
Devon folk always have a smile,
And time to stay and talk a while.
With all this you can see
Why Shaldon means so much to me.

Gillian S Roberts

Fawkland Square

The fall of wings
on a bloodstained arm,
fresh furrows criss-crossing
below a hand holding vodka
rhythmically raised to a scabbed mouth
which once smiled with charm
but is now contorted into a grimace
as the spirit sinks down.

The fusion of feathers
around a tired pair of shoes
a benign peace on a worn face
lightening the grey birds' day
with crumbs from ill-afforded
stale white bread
falling, showering, ground and clothes
amid a flight of feathers.

These two,
sweetly detached in their own worlds
self-contained, self-denied,
or self-indifferent
to the chatter of children
and the urgency of shoppers
on a bright autumnal morning
in Fawkland Square.

R P Avery

Music On The Train

The train pulled out at eight pm
Chaos reigned as passengers, myself included,
Searched for vacant seats; jostling, bumping
And dumping down bags and cases, papers and books.
Staking out their claims.

We had been let on at five to eight!
Well done, oh dismal service. Another farce
Another train, another day. Why is it my carriage
Lies always at the end? My running days are past
I can but pant and hurry.

Yet there were others, slower, older, struggling
A frail old man gripping his wife's hand as
He pulled her along the never-ending platform
Trying to comfort her with kind words
'Don't worry, it won't go, we're nearly there!'

Fortune smiled, a window seat but going backwards
I watched the station shrink until it spun away
Amid the tangled web of lines and sleepers.
Shabby buildings dissolving
In failing light and clinging drizzle.

I dozed and woke to someone's beeping watch
Vague shapes of trees and fields drifted past
Turning one's eyes back to fellow travellers
Tired, bored, unsmiling, silent but for
Coughs and wheezes and clunking lap-top keys.

Weariness overtook me once again, and in my sleep
A tenor sang, a melody so rich and pure I felt at peace
My eyelids lifted of their own accord
To see across the aisle, a young man, ears plugged in,
Singing from a Mozart score.

John Brooks

THE BEACH

The beach is nice,
I love it so much,
it was just made,
with a finger touch.

The sea is blue,
and as cold as ice,
a stony base,
full sand would be nice.

The sand is soft,
as light as can be,
comfortable enough,
for you and me.

The wind is mean,
can be bitterly cold,
makes you shiver,
and feelings go bold.

Julie Titchener

In Hospital

Once I could run, once I could walk
Once I could laugh, once I could talk
Just once too often I took a dare
Then I was young without a care

All at once I have grown up
No more am I a young pup
The car was speeding much too much
Now here I lay I have no sense of touch

Across the road I would run
To me it seemed so much fun
It seemed to me an innocent game
Now they tell me I am lame

More than this I will never walk
Although in time I may learn to talk
I feel so helpless lying here
Excuse me if I shed a tear

Pauline Friend

BRIGHT SCARF

I am not a flower
Approach with care
Beat your wings and wonder
Land - if you dare

I am not a flower
How could I be?
You don't impress - you can't
terrorise me

I'm looking at the 'lions
speckling the lawn
So much has gone to seed
forsaken - forlorn

I used to be a child
here in this place
Together we have aged -
devoid of grace

There is no stale salute
to offer now
I wear another suit
another gown

I am not a flower
nor ever was:
I weep upon the stairs
for all I've lost

S Greenhalgh

SHORELINE

All is calm as the moonlight
Kisses the water, this mirrored night
Glistens with silver serenity
And I listen as the tide hypnotises me.
Each placid wave that laps the shore
Draws back then licks the sand once more,
And the 'Sea Princess' tied at the quay
Like an infant's cradle she bobs and sways
To and fro
On the ebb and flow.
As this great sea breathes so deep
It sighs the rhythm of tranquil sleep.
Each gentle motion soothes me
As this mighty ocean moves me.

Alison Glithro

Upon The Hillside

Sitting in my log cabin, watching the sun's bright light,
dancing upon the stream reflecting the beauty of the world.
The white fluffy clouds, like marshmallows on a fire,
absorbing this sight shall fill any heart's desire.

The mountains topped with pink icing,
the delicious green streams,
Closing your eyes, it feels like a dream,
running in the decorated fields, with yellow and green grass.

Dancing upon the hillside you discover how to laugh,
feeling the winds gently telling their tales,
as the golden sun's light discovers the soft purple heather,
hiding, dancing beneath the lush green grass.

If only everyone could see this beauty inside our world,
maybe they should join me in my log cabin
. . . upon the hillside.

Nadia Darwish

TURN TAIL

I knew a haunted house where we went to be scared many years ago,
That stood on a hill with bleak sickly walls,
And gaping black narrow windows.
We'd creep on our bellies through bare turnip fields,
And hide crouched down in tall grass
by the light of the moon full and pale,
Reflecting in dark shattered glass.
In girt-up loins we could crawl really close
with chattering teeth and clattering bones
and look for the ghoul who we knew lurked in there,
For we'd all seen it drifting loose limbed up the stairs,
And heard rusty chains dragging behind, his raggy old garments,
All stinky with grime.
But should ever we see his long hollow face,
We'd vanish ourselves, never leaving a trace,
And go back tomorrow - well - we weren't really scared,
For wasn't our motto, 'He who wins is who dares'.

Valerie Brown

Summer Storm

The obsidian night is drenched in sweat.
Air that can hold no more moisture cries a soft rebellion.
The balmy darkness whispers its anticipation to the slumbering trees -
A gentle warning of the maelstrom to come.
A black and white day flashes, and surrenders again to the
hallowed night.
Nature's flash-gun leaves after-images in my dark-turned eyes -
Painting Gigeresque abstracts in the surreal clouds.
The smallest taste of fear appears in my deepening thoughts,
As my ancient memory awakens from its cellular sleep.
Subsonic and harmonic rumbles lazily rebound in the acoustic air -
A bass drum - its skin the sky:
Struck on the heartbeat of the Great Sky Spirit.

The sun-warmed winds coax and caress the storm closer,
And closer to my fevered face.
The breeze, more insistent now, wipes the sweat from my heated brow -
Cool, sensuous fingers stroking my skin.
My body charges static with energy crackling through my veins
As the lightning pulses ripple and bolt -
Reaching down from the tormented clouds to stroke the expectant earth,
The bass drum strikes a louder peal -
Beating an incitation for the marching legions of cloud and noise.
A bone-rattling, ear-splitting message of our place in the natural order,
And the rains scream their relief to be unlocked from the sky,
And the sky forgives the disruption to its calm countenance -
Sighing with the return of its gentler times.

Sylvia Spence

SLAB SQUARE C 1970

Meet me down the market square, 'tho there is no market there
Shoppers busy to and fro, some will buy and some don't know
Carriers full from C&A, there must have been a sale today
Hardware, clothes, new shoes and books, cosmetics to improve
your looks
Purses sagging, children nagging, *have we finished yet?*
Husbands leer, craving beer, what's left for you to get?

Queues for Corporation bus, correct fare only causes fuss
Ask direction where to go 'turn left here and up Long Row'
No time to look at people round you 'bout how many will astound you
Bargains galore with prices dropping, today's the day to do
your shopping
To and froing, where are we going, we've come by this way twice
Hustle bustle aching muscle, a rest would come in nice

Skinheads gather on the wall, short haircuts some none at all
Turn-ups high above their boots, faded Levi's denim suits
Hari Krishna Friends of Jesus, mini skirts on beauties please us
Hell's Angels' garb in any weather, wearing colours on their leather
Pigeons flapping, cameras snapping, kids upon a lion
Winos stewed, down-beats lewd, the law to keep an eye on

The Flying Horse, Exchange and Bell, dinner time drinkers
there to dwell
Turned out by three and what a sight, can't wait to go back in at night
Exchange Walk hawkers shout the most, between the cries
of E'ening Post
A city day is full and long, amid the Nottinghamian throng
A few quid lent, the rest is spent, less bus fare to go home
So-long to thy fine, symmetrical skyline, so-long to the
Council House dome

Gary Roe

Lady Of The Lake (Llyn Ogwen)

I first saw her by the wild springs
Of the young heather and the briar,
Attending to the sunlight falling
In gowns of flowing fire,
To ripple across the brooding Llyn Ogwen
Like waves of ripened corn.
And when I asked my mother then
About the appearing lady fair,
She replied that I am only seeing
What is no longer there.

And at night she would touch upon me
Against the moonlight's lemon showing
The lady of the silvery lake.
And a soft breeze would be blowing,
Enticing me to come away,
And her beckoning figure would only half turn
Towards my watching way.
Yet something told me in the passing by
That I must never look upon her face again,
But it never told me why.

Norman Royal

NIGHT DELIGHTS

Cliché to say
I prefer you this way.
No tourists, or occasional walkers,
No vendors, or annoying hawkers.
Just me and my footprints
To leave others the hint.
Empty sands stretch before me,
Running away from my memories.
The moon's reflections,
Heralds my expectations.
Waves curl to the sky,
Whilst on wet sand I lie.
Drawing visions of time,
Here will always be mine.

Anna Walker

So Green Is My Valley

Growing up in the valley, when I was young,
black slag and coal tips were all around,
though many birds twittered and sang,
there was not much green on the ground.

It was part of our daily life,
along with trouble and strife,
everything covered with dirt and grit,
even the air seemed to be full of it.

Daily, the clothes were washed clean and spry,
out the back they were hung to dry,
soon they all had to be brought back in,
everything was as 'black as sin'.

The rivers polluted with foam and slime,
trees and flowers all full of dust,
the landscape too was covered in grime,
nothing we could do, accept it we must.

We were glad when winter came,
the landscape was no longer the same,
tips, trees and mountains all covered in snow,
photo's were taken - grand pictures to show.

All too soon the rain would come,
drab once more it was to be seen.
Oh! what a joy it is today,
the valley is now, beautiful and green.

Robert Gerald

The Underground

Buskers in the subways
Playing for a living
Homeless seeking shelter
From weather unforgiving
Hookers on the platforms
Touting for their trade
Scented and alluring
That's how their living's made
Sitting in the carriage
Observing all the faces
Millions of people
Going different places
Businessmen in pin-striped suits
With bowler hats and brollies
Girls in their designer clothes
Old dears with shopping trolleys
People filling crosswords in
People reading books
People sitting opposite
Give each other furtive looks
Tourists from around the world
With cameras round their necks
Multi-coloured clothing
In spots and stripes and checks
If you spend a little time down there
You'll see the world go round
And get a worm's eye view of life
On the Underground.

David R Williams

THE SHOPPING CENTRE

My first day out - I've been in bed
I've really felt quite low
You must get out, the doctor said
Find somewhere to go.

So here I am, inside my car
I prayed I'd find a space
Get out and look around, you fool
My heart begins to race.

There's people milling all around,
How do the old folk cope?
They need someone to help them
Or they would have no hope.

A lift? Oh no, I'll use the stairs
I feel closed in with these
Bright lights and perfume from flower stalls
Mix with hamburgers and cheese

Faces, people, everywhere
It gives me quite a fright
I find a rail, look down and feel
Quite dizzy from the height!

Tables, chairs and hungry folk
There's really quite a queue.
In these strange surroundings
I don't know what to do.

I really meant to get some clothes
I've got the cash to pay
I'm going around in circles though -
I'll try - another day!

Elizabeth Ross

SENSE OF PLACE

Eight and a half weeks in hospital, in a room without a face,
The walls cloaked in winter greens, where dull curtains chase.
Oxygen masks hanging on elastic, bright spotlights overhead,
Sterile gloves in boxes, a white shiny sink and then the bed.
Cold comfort, rock hard and groaning with an empty threat,
Crisp white sheets and blankets, these treats are what you get,
A grey cardboard bedpan nestles in drab wheeled commode,
Waiting, brakes on, for its next sitter needing to unload.
Uniformed nurses hurry in quick succession in and out of rooms
Taking temperatures, feeling pulses, smiling faces never gloom.
Stethoscope, thermometer, scissors, pens and sticky tape in hand
Shiny trays rattle with syringes and things, time I think to disband.
White-coated doctors hastily talking, plenty of yackerty-yak,
Nods of agreement, some writing, a promise and then a cut-back.
Then there's the food to think of, or perhaps you'd rather not,
Meat that smells like dog food and things that really should be hot.
Dried vegetables chopped up like infant foods and custard, well
This must be apple crumble or maybe it's prunes I can't tell.
The theatre's the place that you dread, not full of actors you see,
It's where the surgeons slice and cut and give you blood for free.
Eight and a half weeks in hospital and I think you'll all agree
    that there's plenty of nicer places that I'd rather be.

Amanda Louise Thompson

DUST MITE

Dust mite on a tiny planet,
I tried to catch love
between my thumb and forefinger.
Was it so small
that it slipped away?
I reached out with both hands
to catch love with an embrace.
Was it so big
that it could not be held?

I look from here to the stars,
knowing there are more,
perhaps endless galaxies,
billions and billions of suns.
I wonder: is it like love,
too vast to grasp?

Yet lying here
with you in my arms,
I hold it all:
love, stars, galaxies, the lot.
Dust mite on a tiny planet,
I hold it all.

Jim Powell Hill

BROADSTAIRS BAY

Lazing upon these camel-haired grains
Close to the brine seasoned timber pier
I spy the whitewashed, tufted cliffs
Where the soft warm air puffs fresh and clear.

The broad sweep of this horseshoe bay
Is a generous nest for idle lovers
Where fledglings fly, minds limitless and free
Grasping a joy more satisfying than any other

Gulls hang gracefully upon a thermal breeze
Gliding effortlessly, mocking with their call
Benevolent and omnipresent
These bleak harbour masters watch over one and all

These days are a dreamy semi-halucination
Induced by the hypnotic drone of far-off ships
Here in this place of fish and gulls
I find an insular isle where I can happily exist.

Dave Lunn

I Sensed The Crafts Of Yesteryear

There were many crafts of yesteryear, all done by human hand,
by the dedicated work force, who were the proudest in the land,
The blacksmith at the smithy would shoe and fettle horses' hoofs
while the thatcher with his artistry, created all those fancy roofs.

Transport in those early days, relied upon the horse-drawn cart,
to keep such vehicles on the road, the wheelwright played his part,
he cuts the hub, fits the spokes, and in sections shapes the wheel,
then with strength and perfection, fits on the rim of hardened steel.

Attachments were required, to connect the horse up to the shafts,
all manufactured by the saddler, supreme masters of these crafts,
the harness, girth and collar, the intricate bridal complete with bit,
these parts made to perfection, for they had to be a perfect fit.

Another important country craft, casks and barrels had to be made,
a task performed by the cooper, a man specialised in his trade,
for the brewery it was important, with the need to transport their ales,
to the village inns where craftsmen, over a pint could tell their tales.

The basket maker had an important role, in the rural way of life,
making baskets for the farmers, with willow and a good sharp knife,
their products were of varying size, and used for collecting crops.
The pecking basket for potatoes, and the largest for fruit and hops.

The candle maker of bygone days, was quite a common sight
for at that time not many folk, had access to the electric light,
we also had the potter, who relied solely on pedal power,
making vessels of every type, plus garden pots for any flower.

One final country craftsman, whose numbers get smaller and smaller,
working alone up in the Dales, of course it is the dry-stone waller,
one's senses could depict these crafts, such treasures we must endear,
to keep forever in our memories, the great country crafts of yesteryear.

Wenn-The-Penn

SINGLE BEAUTY

In single beauty there you lie,
Sweet and lonely, but oh so fie.
Did some tiny wing of sweetly singing robin bring
A gentle breeze or mighty gale
Bring you to this silent dale,
Which ere maybe, much joy is mine
As I gaze upon your form divine,
Tonight I'll dream of you sweet flower
As you sleep alone in your lonely bower

Patricia Madden

POSTNATAL SEPARATION

Nurses pass
and urgent whispers dance
on antiseptic waves
I weep
as darkness creeps around
and wins

Crushed, deplete
I wake and hear
your scream
am caught

You're gone
to brittle, plastic womb
mere walls away
I fight
but shadows, neatly parked
fly down
no pre-paid tomb
more desolate

I weep
such vast despair
your floodlit terror
separate
our joining cut, undone
was nearer
than can ever be again

I hear your scream
mere walls away
but cannot rise
I call
but no-one comes

Shirley Frost

A BETTER PLACE?

As I walk along the corridor
feeling like an empty shell
the plain white walls around me
and the disinfectant smell
I listen to the silence
shattered only by my shoe
I feel that I should creep
on my way to visit you
I walk into the private room
I sit upon the bed
I pray that you will move
Just slightly turn your head
I glare at the machines surrounding you
I know they hold your life
but life will have no meaning
if I cannot be your wife
I glance around the room
roses fill the air
but I don't even see them
as I sit with my despair
slowly your eyes flicker
I hear the birds, I touch your face
suddenly life's much brighter
Yes, the world's a lovely place.

Joy Benford

THE SCHOOL

I walked around the old school,
Not a child was there in sight.
It was so very early morning,
Not even daylight.

I stood alone - centre of the hall,
And listened to echoes of the past.
I could smell the polish on the floor,
How long would this peace last.

The hall was very old you see,
Even older than the school;
Years ago it had been the only room,
Where children were told - obey the rule.

This place had known some happy times,
And sadness, I have no doubt.
It gave me such a feeling of happiness,
When I looked around and about.

On one wall was a list so sad,
Of pupils killed in the war,
The rest were decorated with
Children's work - more and more.

My school was such a happy place,
No 'our' school I should say;
Because it belonged to all of us,
And always will - in every way.

At last the door burst open,
And a little voice said to me,
'Am I too early - outside shall I wait?'
'Why no, my dear, how could you be?'

Dorothy Whitehall

PUESTA DEL SOL

Silver shafts cutting cumulus,
Adding texture to the living sky,
Sun sliding behind another cordillera,
Oozing over irregular peaks.

Orange carpet spreading like spilt paint,
Over an ochre landscape and green trees,
Washing mist clinging to the
Mountainside in a clean citrus light.

Scattered green and white houses
Glazed in rainbow dipped glow,
Stained red by reflections of
The end of something beautiful.

Inflamed eye of the dying day
Blinking bloody, burning out,
Like a memory of love,
Fading, fading, fading, gone.

David Atkinson

Heaven Is In The Northern Hills

Heaven is in the northern hills! The only place where I,
Could live for all eternity, and never wish to die.
The wind is fresh; the air is clear, and bouquets like fine wine.
The sun and rain are welcome both. This land I claim as mine!

Heaven is in the northern hills; by northern rivers too,
That rushing, tumble downwards adding drama to the view.
Tees and Tyne with Tweed and Tay, all full of life and flowing.
With massive force each sweeps its course to get to where it's going.

The Peaks, The Dales, The Lake District, and most of Scotland too,
Boast landscape having everything that ever me or you
Could need to heal a broken life, to ease the pain and hurt,
And shift the other baggage that comes free with city dirt.

The dynamic that created it, is in the people too.
They don't cry about bad weather until the sun breaks through.
They have to work for all they get, with muscle, not with mouth.
Unlike the effete and indolent, who occupy the south.

The greatest British poets: composers, dramatists as well,
Mostly hail from the north country where the soul of man must dwell.
Even a great like Elgar, while an asset to his nation,
Had to roam the Yorkshire Dales to seek his inspiration.

All the best films; best comedy; performers of most worth,
Are without doubt, you must agree, the children of the north.
Yes! Heaven is in the northern hills, the only place where I
Could live for all eternity and never wish to die.

Knutsson

THE SHORE

I stand on the shore, and look out to sea.
A lighthouse on an island, shines its light to me.
I hear the ocean roar, and a gull screech in the air -
Maybe it's found some food, or maybe it's lost in despair.
I smell sea salt, in the mist,
And the stench of seaweed, with a revolting twist.
Then I see a fisherman, digging for worms,
He looks inside his bucket, then he turns.
I see a speedboat, heading for the pier,
And to the right, she does steer.
I see brown clay cliffs, with grass at the top,
A rabbit comes out of a hole, does a jump and then a hop.
I stand here alone, in this crescent bay -
And here a little longer, I think I'll stay.

Samantha Douglas (12)

FIRE

Silent insidious flames, so destructive,
Eating away in the dead of night.
All consuming.
Licking up walls, dancing across cupboards.
Continuously searching for escape, fighting captivity.
Transforming material objects beyond recognition.
Searing, charring, melting disfiguring.
Greedily feeding its insatiable hunger
Outwards spreading from its original source.
Living, evil entity with unquenchable thirst.
Unfeeling uncaring, so totally selfish
Belching noxious fumes, dense and black.
Wreaking havoc, erasing, destroying memorabilia.
Claiming lives, inflicting trauma, injuring souls.
Leaving in its wake trails of smouldering devastation
Blackened remains of a once beautiful home.

Teresa Booth

THE LIGHTHOUSE

A spider-like gantry
stretches its legs across from
beam to beam of
driftwood hewn planking
suspended solidly above the
powder-grey sand as soft as
grit between the toes

Gleaming dully a
large brass plaque stands
screwed into the far side of the
structure,
slightly above eye-level,
and as the group strain
to read the legend
one stumbles and has to
be caught by
the arm

Further up the lighthouse
there is a set of double doors
alien white in colour
with a consistency of
flesh

Behind them there is a child
running

Martin Edmonds

SEA SIGNS

Shells and smells,
Waves and caves,
Gulls and hulls.

Colossal cliffs,
Pounding pebbles,
Stunning starfish.

Beaches of beauty,
And spectacular seas,
Your senses saturated and teased.

The sight of sun-worshippers,
The smell of seaweed,
The touch of tentacles,
The taste of tuna fish,
The sound of seagulls.

A beautiful place,
Upon this earth's face.

Signs of the sea,
And all are free.

C Shadwell

Hidden Valley

Far from unseeing eyes
There lies in this land
Many unplanned surprises
A hidden valley
Home to Goannas, Cockys and Roos
Sunshine and storms
Mother nature doth supply
Corners of rock
Trees that reach up to the sky
People come to settle
On the land
Calling each place their home
Plant their flowers
Work that comes
From their very souls
Once you have seen this hidden valley
Deciding to call it home
Never more will you ever wish to roam.

P M Lightfoot

Cliffs Of County Clare

I stood,
On a clifftop,
Facing the wild
And overwhelming
Broad Atlantic Ocean,
Looking westward
Into the far distance,
Listening to the blustering wind,
And watching the spray
Flung heavenwards
In supplication,
And the white
Churning water,
Eddying around the rocks;
My mind wondering
At nature's force,
And seeing
The powerful,
Rugged beauty,
Of the cliffs of Moher
In County Clare.

H Val Horsfall

TALL-SHIPS

The tall-ships came slowly into view
Rigging, manned by a capable crew.
As they sailed by the Bass Rock,
This was surely the finest sailing stock!

Majestic, quaint travel from the past,
Ships made to last by masters of their craft,
The main sail rigged at the ready,
Onward, with the wind 'Steady boys, steady'

My mind wandered back to tales of yore
When pirates plundered - all in store
Silks, spices, tobacco, cotton, riches galore
Slaves, chained and whipped in the holds below.

How peacefully they sailed, no sign of trouble
Crew willing, able, ready at the double.
What an experience in a lifetime to see
These majestic tall-ships sail across the sea!

Maisie Roberts

The Ring Of Kerry

Earlier this year we went to the Emerald Isle,
It took a long time because it was many a mile,
We boarded a ferry to cross the Irish Sea,
Leaving in the early hours to get there for tea,
And settling down in our holiday home
With map in hand we planned to roam.

The Ring of Kerry looked good in the book,
So we agreed we would go there and take a look,
Driving to Killarny seemed to take hours,
Sometimes through sun sometimes through showers,
When we got there we picked up the sign,
Lakes and mountains we hoped to find.

The first sign we saw was for the waterfall,
It was hidden behind trees so green and so tall,
We walked up the path we could hear the sound,
Of thunderous water falling to the ground,
White water cascading off the top,
Racing over rocks never to stop.

Back in the car we started to climb,
Passing lakes, rocks and trees of pine,
We arrived at a place called Ladies View,
Looking down the mountain with lakes peeping through,
This beautiful sight is hard to conceive,
It has to be seen to be believed.

Dingle Peninsula was our next port of call,
And the sighting of another white waterfall,
More mountains and sea as onward we went,
Back to Killarny from where we were sent,
The Ring of Kerry we will hold dear to our hearts,
Memories of the Emerald Isle never to part.

Celia Law

CHANGING SCENES

In the wood a stillness
Hazy mist through filtered light.
A ribbon path, moss covered banks
Grace this trail on either side.

Deep among the trees a changing scene
Sounds now pervade the air.
Rustle of leaves, small creatures emerge
And deer like statues, halt and stare.

Through the wood I retrace my steps
Once more the silence unfolds
As though a 'secret' it conceals
Which will always remain 'untold'.

Betty M Varley

CHANGES

Once there were hedgerows
And fields freshly furrowed,
Foxes in lairs
And rabbits in burrows,
Wild flowers edging the country lanes
Farmers fastidiously sowing their grain.
Once cows grazed peacefully
Where the grass grew so lush,
While the music of birdsong
Flowed freely from the bush.

Once dry-stone dykes
Framed the haystacks and barns,
And the imprint of tractor tyres
Led to the farms.
Scents of the seasons - unique and unspoiled
Relaxing the senses - like a spring being uncoiled.
So oft has this ground
Kissed the soles of my feet,
With steps firm in success
And unsure in defeat.

Now I search for that scene
Perplexed! In confusion!
I blink - and it's gone.
Was it all an illusion?
New houses have appeared like toadstools in the grass
Breeding profusely as did rabbits in the past.
No longer the greenery,
Peace and tranquillity.
But 'twill always be there,
For me - in my memory.

Christine Kelly

Palace Style

Sculptures and portraits.
Words woven to retain the past on walls,
Books of massive volumes.
Brocades of diverse manufacturers,
Linens and heavy curtains,
This is a different place!
Its setting conveys the message,
And there the maidens in their flarey attire,
Busy themselves life to bring to this monument.

Soft raiment and soft shoes,
Graceful movements of cultured life.
Set hairs by professional experts,
Perfection seems paramount here.
As yet life here as this place conveys
Is filled with protocols and set rules to honour,

And why not
The head needs be an example.
The influx demands the high standard,
And those who live in palace glory
Should exhibit but a self-giving
Life to the mass.

Stairs in flight as the east is to the west,
Rooms of diverse decoration in display,
Carpets of red colours depicting sovereignty
And blue colours of royal descent.
Tapestry and art in perfect order arranged
And yet these in relation to heaven's glory
Only go as far as the eye can see.

Tina Nyamebah Edwards

ISLAND

Starting its final descent the plane banks gently round
till I can see the tiny clustered houses
starkly white against the black volcanic ground.
A fiery sun strikes sparks upon the surface of a
deep aquamarine sea and as machinery brings us down to earth
I watch the natural beauty of a seagull soaring free.

Anticipated heat, bright and intense still takes me
by surprise making me gasp and lift a hand to shield
my dazzled eyes.
On twisting roads, through barren hills, thirsty and brown
until at last we reach the jumbled streets of the old town
where bougainvillaeas spill like purple waterfalls and
sweet hibiscus paint their vivid friezes round old
whitewashed walls.
It feels like home.
I've always been contented in this place
where everyone I meet smiles from a seemingly familiar face.
Perhaps reincarnation is, in fact, a mystic truth
and in some former life eons ago I've spent my youth
or lived out my old age here on this sunny isle.
For now - it saddens me to know that I can only stay
so short a while.
But I'll return as I have done before time and again
drawn by a kind of longing,
a need I can't explain.

Pat Cooper

Reality

I want to go home
to the place I once knew
where the grass is still green
and the sky is still blue.
Though the people I knew
have left long ago
it's the place that I want
not the people I know.
For it's there that my heart
longs to retreat
where the air is still fresh
and the memories still sweet.
So each night as I sleep
on a carpet I fly
back to the place I once
left, high and dry
oh, so long ago.

A J Marshall

The Shallows

Into naught but shallows shall I spread the sea
Mere layers deep and smooth as air
No drowning void no ragged spray
Quiet light expanding to darkless horizons
In every part of the shallows will I be
In every breath of sky will I glide
In every grit of sand will I dream
Unmoving on a tranquil song of tides

Jose Lacey

THE LABURNUM TREE

(1950, aged 3)

At the end of our lawn
On the left-hand side
Grew a golden laburnum tree.
Beneath, a blue mist of forget-me-nots,
A magic place for me.

And one summer day
My mother and I
Sat under the glowing tree:
She made me a crown of golden flowers -
No Queen more Royal then Me.

Jennifer Bailey

SCUNTHORPE

I remember, in the east, the glow
Of dawn at midnight on the long horizon
Where the furnaces stood tall; and I remember
The mushroom cloud erupting in the afternoon
From the sinter plant, depositing red dust
On terraced houses and straight suburban streets,
Leaving a film on every windowsill
And settling, like foraminifera on the sea-bed,
On the grey repetitions of the rooftops.

Stan Downing

SUMMER SEASON

The summer season has begun
Tourists here seeking the sun
They throng along the esplanade
Students in groups jet along
'Merci Combien' the French will say
When on the pier they pay
For ice-cream cornets, lemon drinks
Or candyfloss, pink, on sticks
People in deckchairs sit
Upturned faces, women who knit
Men with paunches on their haunches
Sprawling, snoring in the sun
Barking dogs go bounding by
Shaking their coats as bodies lie
Oily, sweating, lobster red
As the wet droplets spread
A black and white terrier stands
Staring, blinking in the sun
Hoping to scrounge chicken, or bun
A woman hollers at her charge
Will you stop throwing stones
If you don't you're going home
Anyway the sun is low, stop grissling
Give your nose a blow!

V Brickley

A Walk By The Canal

A stroll we said to talk
But bearing witness of our soul
Is the canal as we walk.
Each disorient
Want to return from whence
In fear each rising its fence
Debating on obeying sense
A small boat row along,
In tune the water spirits
Sing their song
Rhythmical I touch your hand.
My heart become sinking sand
Gently you squeeze my hand
In a notion that you understand
Each feeling the other weakness
Spontaneously we head to the bench.
A kiss confirming our destiny
To the canal and ourselves.

Carol Barrett

The Abbey Ruins

Once this was a thriving community
living in peace, love and unity.
Sanctuary sought and given direct,
bound by honour, held in respect.

A simple life of work and prayer,
animal husbandry done with care.
Fruit and vegetables grown each year,
bee in hive, fish in mere.

Then the king made his resolve,
the monasteries he did dissolve.
Across the land the army thundered
buildings razed their contents plundered.

Through the centuries the wind has blown,
and men have used the scattered stone.
For house or farm, road or shed,
in ancient footsteps we live and tread.

Foundation stones mark out where
the altar stood accepting a prayer.
Fingers of stonework point to the sky,
crumbling pillars in grass do lie.

From the past the ghost and echoes
in peace and calm around us flows.
And wraps us in a cloak of love,
past and present, hand in glove.

In silent awe we stand and gaze,
time can't diminish or erase
the holy feeling of prayer and hymn,
from here the goodness will never dim.

Barbara Fitzgerald

HAPPY DAYS

My heart was filled with happy hours,
Bluebell woods, and pretty flowers,
Walking through meadows, of grass so green,
The loveliest sight, you've ever seen.

Resting by a bubbling brook,
Reading poems, from a book,
Love and happiness, comes to mind,
When all these pleasures, I do find.

Slowly walking down the hill,
Everything so quiet, and still,
Until I reached a cottage small,
When as a child, I did recall.

There were roses round the door,
Where memories linger, for evermore.
I lifted the latch, and what did I see,
A welcome there, waiting for me.

Two pink cheeks, and arms open wide,
As I closed the door, and went inside.
The warmth of the fire, burning bright,
A cat sitting there, as black as night.

What fond memories, there were here,
Of loved ones, always and ever dear,
And so my thoughts, go on and on,
Of folk who lived here, long since gone.

Win

Edge Of The Rain

When brilliant skies once put asunder
Bring passion in crying tears of rain.
And steaming water touches clouds,
Forming mists over islands, my islands.
Where green rocks in piping whirlpools
Are splendid and searching;
And basking sharks are seen lurching,
These tides flourishing in moods of colour.
I see my soul on this coasted plain,
Where ancestors brood on the edge of the rain.

Intrepid fisher lads baffle the wind
As Celtic magicians blow sand on their sails.
'How goes it, Captain?' 'Wet!', he spells,
As skuas swoop and purchase steal.
He loves the waves, and so do I,
His clan so steeped in aqua lore.
I sense them watching, so does he.
He hails the mysteries of the sea,
And feeds its power, feeling pain
As mists approach the edge of the rain.

These clouds are wondrous, big and brash,
And yet they cannot fill this hole in the sky.
I wonder why, as seething water hits my beach,
That storms and seas and offshore crags
Are treasures stored in heaven's hold.
And I know where I'm from - it must be here.
So I raise my hand and finger the sun,
And I smile at the brae of the land.
If the history of the isles is in my brain,
Then my eye must pursue the edge of the rain.

S Peter Robson

The Ideal End

The annual carnival was fun as it paraded along the prom;
then warmed by the setting sun, the ideal way to end the day
was a walk along the sands. Chasing around rockpools;
making footprints; squidging lugworm castes; finding shells.
Tiny children can't resist feeling with their hands.

Next time can we bring a bucket? The youngest one implores.
From beach to illuminated glen and through to the waiting car,
is more exciting via lighted dinosaurs and fairy glens.
An ideal evening's end. All such good memories so far.

Home again, bedtime excitement passes, and on into the night,
First one child and then the other two are suddenly stricken
by a violent sickly plight. Grab bucket, bath, sink and loo -
anything watertight will do! Washing machine's on night-shift.

Did you walk along the beach? Our doctor asked next day,
There's a nasty bug there - a real bacterial peach, he said.
He told how, for all the poor children with beach-touching-blues,
the cure was quick and easy: just antibiotics, rest and bed.

Yes, the carnival was grand. The walk was an ideal end - but
you'll need a bucket (and a doctor) if li'l fingers touched the sand!

So every time we drive past the bay our youngest child
cannot understand: Why? She will moan and groan and cry.
Why? Why can't she walk? Paddle? Dig or play? *Sorry - No Way!*
No matter how sunny, dry, or warm and pleasant the day.

Yes, one thing here is certain: the ideal end in every way -
Only the sewage and the seagulls can go on the beach and stay!

Christine Thomas

A Special Lure

My feet submerged deep below the sand,
as I watched the waves,
crash on the rocks,
and the sun set high in the sky,
as the crabs shuffle by,
causing soft knocks.

I could see with my ears,
and hear with my eyes,
I didn't know I would feel
this way,
I didn't realise.

I had a sense of déjà vu,
but I'd never seen a sight
as beautiful as this before.
To me,
it seemed to have a special lure.

Danielle Linton

ROTTINGDEAN 1997

On a brief winter visit to Rottingdean
The village pond spruced up and freshly cleaned
And just but a short stone's throw away
A hundred years ago to this day.

The house where Rudyard Kipling lived and stayed
Its walled gardens safe from winds and salty spray
I walked its crumbly old brick paths
For they were my stairway to the past.

Of when smugglers' horses still trotted by
With kegs of brandy disembarked at Rye
When tall ships still sailed the seven seas
Awaiting each and every ocean breeze.

The peace, the tranquillity did they inspire to write
For in these gardens still blooms the winter aconite
As I sit in the shelter of the old summer house
Sitting there silently as quiet as a mouse.

Forgetting the traffic that thunders on by
Along the coastal road that leads to Rye
The horseless carriage, the twentieth century reality
Gone forever the bygone days of tranquillity.

Dennis Jenkinson

THE CHERRY ORCHARD

How wonderful that garden was
In the heat of a summer's day.
The cherries ripe around our heads
As we ran out to play.

We picked the fruit of shining red
And in our mouths it went.
The taste of sweet, creamy flesh abound,
The cherries heaven sent.

Strawberries too were ours to gather
From the yellow straw.
The first ones eaten in a second,
Our fingers gathering more.

At lunchtime cold meat to eat,
Served with salad from the garden.
Then a dish of new minted potatoes,
From cool larder taken.

When summer skies had faded
And the air was warm,
We'd all stroll along to the
Local pub for lemonade on
The lawn.

Our one big treat was fish
And chips from a mobile van.
The delicious taste stayed in
Our mouths as down the streets
We ran.

Poppy Ashfield

Hill Of Gold

Like a sentinel, silent and still,
Stanford Church looks out from a hill.
With gravestones standing all around,
Swathed in gold across the ground.

Quietly sat upon a bench,
That's hard to leave and such a wrench.
Whilst admiring the local views,
I sit silent and just muse.

Only a breeze shakes each head,
Of the daffodils above the dead.
Here amongst this hill of gold,
Unspoilt, untouched this scene so bold.

Daisies, violets, primroses too,
Look at me from between each shoe.
Apart from now this hill is green,
When you'd not know, that spring had been!

Susan Green

ISTANBUL MAY 1997

Istanbul where east meets west
Is full of noise and motion.
People team from everywhere,
The air full of commotion.
Mosques and minarets reach the sky
And really are impressive
The markets bustle, the whole place throbs
And can be quite aggressive.
Colours smell and sounds bombard,
My senses are sent whirling.
The water gleams and boats glide past,
The scenes are so alluring.
This city is just so exciting
The streets and sites are most inviting.
The food is good, the transport easy
But sometimes leaves you feeling queasy!
Taxis dashing in and out
You cross the road, but please watch out!
A sense of history all around,
Impressions left are quite profound.
I'm glad I came to see it all
To see the colours, hear the calls
Of mullahs in the mosques around -
Your shoes remove its holy ground.
Yes Istanbul's a place to see.
I hope you'll go and will agree!

Gill Kipps

I Wandered Lonely As A Child

I wandered lonely as a child
across river-bank and streams,
the place, where towering spires smiled
and there beneath branches welcome shade,
I shared my broken dreams.
beyond canal's locked gate; watching
the world thro' broken blue glass,
escaped reality's sad tomb.
Curled up by reeds hidden in grass,
dreams of other pleasant things; safe
within its motherly womb, essence of man
that, in the river of life; together swims.

On such journeys, would run away
my troubled tear-stained face,
fascinated by all that nature had on display,
by rivers' soothing pace, where swollen eyes
could bathe in beautiful scenery.
Walk ancient viaducts, built by Roman hands
unwavering lines of brick set in greenery
gigantic arches raised like palms,
spread across pleasant fields, of better times,
safe, where nature nursed me, in her arms.

I made my home, where forest's shady wood
had shown me tenderness; its
earthen heart did me good,
memories where refreshing stream caressed
a cloud of bluebells in May.
Its faded blue-green carpet
now lay: a fallen wilderness.
Nature's heart then lovingly given
in my lonely childhood smiled,
stronger now, by her gifts, am shriven
I wander, a lonely poet, as nature's child.

Mary Jayne Evans

DREAMLAND. BUS 7. STAND E

Take this bus to dreamland
Fear for what waits there.
Make an effort step inside
You'll only need the fare.

Behind his wheel the driver sits
Grinning from ear to ear.
Brush the cobwebs from his door
Let him know you're here.

Sit down at a window seat
Watch as scenes pass by.
If he drives down memory lane
It'll only make you cry.

The bus ride is through mind-land
Slough and utter despair.
Feel love's passion and its pain
Your wife is waiting there.

She left you by an early bus
The choice it wasn't hers.
You kissed her fondly on cold lips
Whilst Angels paid her fare.

Dawn light 'waken the morning sky
Another day breaks clear.
Brings you closer to the heart
Of one that you hold dear.

Life's journey once begun
Through its laughter, joy and tears.
Cry 'Stop the bus the dream is done'
The terminus is here.

Francis B Rylance

The Geriatric Ward

In this desperate, dreary place
Frail souls and mortality come face to face.
Melancholy hangs everywhere
A pervading atmosphere of despair.
Decaying mounds lie entombed
Their life in decline, their future doomed.
Fettered, imprisoned, bars secured
No escape until death is assured.
From this cell there is no reprieve
Except when mourners come to grieve.
When dreaded night creeps morbidly
And shrouds the condemned in captivity,
Come tears and moans and groans profane
From wretches who'll not see morn again.
The fearsome night drags on and on
Some battles are lost and some are won.
No difference now, all just the same.
Age unites inmates at the imminent grave.
And visitors who come to weep
Will find they're haunted in their sleep
With memories of pathetic wrecks
Robbed of dignity and respect.
And of those confined without friend or kin
To soothe the longing ache within.
Of shuffling creatures all forlorn
Racked with pain, so bravely born.
Vacant eyes that see no more
Rotting flesh and sagging jaw.
Sadly they watch life ebb away
Towards the awesome judgement day.

Patricia Jamieson

Brighton Wakes Up

Forms floating along in breezes of unison,
Shades of temporary utopia fuse jangled nerves,
Magical light graces the blessed and the tortured
Without bias.

Happy dialogue trips from lover to lover
Unfettered by those routine constraints,
Bodies released from winter's dull drapery,
Skin gains a healthy texture.

Time appears to slow, smiles appear with ease
Budding fillies dance to the rhythm of a new-found freedom,
Strapping colts strip off to parade their tribal markings,
While the office-bound are full of stifled dreams.

Windows become open spaces,
Plants sigh as the sprinklers liquidly caress,
Old folk are embraced by images of distant summers
As if only yesterday, they relax and enjoy.

Matthew W Jones

MIND TRAVELS

Walking in the darkness, through the corridors of time,
To the left and to the right, lay the doorways of my mind,
I sense a deep desire, but yet a stabbing fear,
My footsteps echo in my heart, my fate is drawing near.
Turning to my left I find an old but unlocked door,
It opens with a rusty creak, to show what came before.
I see my life from childhood, and all my teenage years,
To my marriage and my children, and all my hopes and fears.
I close the door behind me and carry on my way,
Another door was there to show the present, now, today.
This door I'll leave unopened, I do not want to see
The things that I had done today, they were still fresh to me.
Suddenly I see a glowing light from a door so strangely new,
I only have to open it and my future'd be in view.
I stand in hesitation, my heart is beating fast,
All the things I hope will be, I might see at last.
But while I stand here frozen, the door bursts open wide,
I suddenly shut tight my eyes, to avoid what is inside,
Then I wake in sudden panic, for I didn't want to see
The future as an open book, showing what's in store for me.

Jayne Jenkins

FLESH SHOP

Impaled on metal S's
Amputations hang.
Headless bodies. Bodiless legs.
While behind glass on serried trays
Necks and breasts are displayed.

White coated and straw boatered
He whistles as he rinses blades,
First red then pink the running water.
The cleaver cleansed. He takes aim -
His practised stroke deep and neat.
Above him a poster exclaims
'Eat more meat!'

Stephen Bone

Take A Look Around

Tick-tock goes the clock
Hanging on the wall
Reflecting back the light
From the mirror in the hall

A chair against the table
A red and brown mat
I wonder why it is
It never lies down flat

A cushion on the sofa
An ornament on the side
All the family photos
Laid out in such pride

A shine upon the brasses
A picture upon the TV
It was taken some six years ago
It's of my husband and of me

A pen upon a book
Lying next to the phone
A ball is on the floor
Next to the dog's play bone

I'm just describing what I see
As I take a look around
It goes to show that all about
Poetry is found.

Barbara D Grindy

Winter's Wings

In silent wonder lies the snow
Crisp white threads begin to sew
Weaving snowflakes from the sky
Falling like frosted butterflies

Blankets of creamy snow lay still
Untouched. Falling as it wills
Floating, forming veils of ice
Glistening there. Children enticed

Crystal cinders sparkle sure
Frosted branches reach for more
Intricate snowflakes, feather light
Dance on the wind that fills the night

Winter's cast her wings for sure
Till morning comes and snow does thaw
Melting 'neath the cheerful sky
Winter's wings have taken flight.

Deborah Hickson

My Home

My house is old, my body too
My bills are high, my pence are few,
But I see the morning.

The trees are bare, the sun is spare
The grass all wet, no worms out there
But I hear the birds, sing in the morning.

I am rich, I am warm
A roof above my head
Some milk to drink
A loaf of bread
My hopes are high in the morning.

My memories, my garden
My animals, what better place
Could I wish for.

D M Haworth

The Need

You should have sensed the feeling, felt the atmosphere,
It brought a lump into the throat, to the eye it brought a tear.
I'm talking of the show, that was performed last week.
If you didn't see it you really missed a treat,
It told the story of Jesus, His birth, death and resurrection,
How He lived His earthly life, lived it to perfection.
People came to hear the story, came from far and wide
Christians and non-believers, standing side by side.
Many folk have turned their back on the church
But they still have a need,
Maybe in our own small way, we have sown a seed.
They listened to the music and the message that was told
It's still needed just as much today
Even though it's 2,000 years old.

Betty Dobson

THE SOMERSET LEVELS

The gate upon the moor was new,
With white bars bright amidst thin haze,
Damp autumn mists had veiled the sun,
As I leant musing, fields before.
A flickering butterfly alone
Was all the movement of that day,
The distant cattle had not stirred,
Nor leaf, nor bird, had passed me by.
Mute rhyne stretched stagnant either side,
Its green bright weed a carpet lay,
Sealing beneath the life within.
So secret hid the carp below,
Known only to wild rush and reed
Hugging the bank in natural pride,
Tall stems with velvet cylinders,
And whispering grasses floating free.
Such ancient willows lined the course,
Deep-scored with barks like rigid stone,
Mere memories of their woven past,
Medieval Merlins, gnarled, benign.
In filtered sunlight through fine gauze,
The timeless moors evoked the past.
Breathless it waits, this fading land,
Whilst herons in slow motion glide.

Carol Exten-Wright

Burial Of A Beggar Man

Noonday in India on banks of the 'Ganges'.
Sultry heat rises like an eagle, and a
gentle calm unveils itself.

A 'Beggar Man' wafer-thin, wrapped in
sackcloth, awaits his funeral pyre.
The solitary mourner, mind in turmoil,
stares at sweating 'pyre man' hewing
wood with calm rhythmic strokes.

A tender breeze drifts from the mountain,
escorting white 'Temple Flowers' which
repose on the fast decaying body.

In the distance dogs howl, cocks crow,
Holy Men chant, and the bustling
life of India moves onward.

Curling, coiling pyre smoke mingles
with sweet sandalwood, and the body
is consumed in hungry flames.
Now the pauper's soul is cleansed forever.

Scarlet ashes, hot and angry, hiss when
fed to the Holy River, and swiftly devoured
by monsoon swollen waters.

Alex Branthwaite

La Tour Jeanne D'Arc, Rouen

Rouen: a name
That echoing mournfully
Casts like a spectral web
Over the banality of its streets
Its pall of shame.

In sunset glow I trod those streets,
Glimpsed ahead that fateful Tower where lay
In iron cage the saintly Maid
Till led in macabre pageant
To the stake.

The Tower loomed in grim portent
As if from out a living tapestry
And into that dark canvas,
Into a moment of terror,
Blackly etched in Time,
In chill foreboding I was drawn.

From phantom windows
Peered a million eyes; upon my ear
Broke, like the furtive hiss
Of waves lashing the pebbled shore,
The murmur or a crowd half-crazed by fear;
From unearthly bournes
Beyond the flame-streaked sky,
Half-muffled in the smoke
Fouling the vernal air,
The chant of priests,
The clank of armour, stamp of hooves,
Harsh trumpets braying out their deadly call . . .

. . . And did I stand that day upon this spot
Five hundred years ago, in Rouen?

Betty Everson

Ring Of Stones

I'm waiting at the centre of your beginning,
Encircled by your ancient strength,

'Speak to me, speak to me.'

My eyes are closed flooding fire,
Shapes of surprise dance across my eyes.
A moon-washed sun soaks feebly into the skin I wear,
A cooling breath plays in my hair.

'Speak to me, speak to me. Tell me your Secret.
Whisper to me, engulf me, give *birth* to me, here
In the rain scented breeze, before the hidden stars,
Before the tiny creatures
Scuttling across your gritty surface.

Let the life clinging to your crevices
Be my witness!

Bear me, lift me up to your soul,
Take me to the Secret,
Make *me* the *Secret!*'

Carole Anne Johnson

Cattle Market

Visiting the cattle market makes me depressed.
Watching the innocent faces of sheep, cows, calves, and pigs, I guess.
Then I feel extremely guilty, thinking of steaming joints,
Accompanied by mint-sauce, stuffing, cranberry, do you get my point?
Cramped in small spaces in stink and filth,
Would you like it? Can't help, but feel guilt.

We are eating far too much meat.
During the war it was a rarity, and a treat!
These creatures must feel, this cattle-place is best not seen.
Being stamped here, a ring put in the ear,
Pushed by them men, to get you, they are keen.

Unforeseen future and destiny,
For them no happiness till eternity.
Their life is planned and made short.
They haven't got a choice or say of sort.

Annemarie Poole

A Vista Of White

Wandering over the windswept dale
That poignant February day.
I followed the curve of the River Dove
To see a vista of white
In the limpid daylight
Stretching far and away.

Wild snowdrops in profusion,
Fresh as a virginal bride.
Rhythmically danced
As I stood entranced
Along the brooding hillside.

Winter was easing her icy grip
As spring painted a natural decor.
A cool white panorama
Breathtaking in it's drama
As they performed their yearly encore.

Pamela Sears

Thoughts On A Garden

The moon shone full tonight,
And I felt sick and estranged,
Along with the cats and cabbages,
In this solemn moonlit garden
Of thistle-weeds and rocks.

Like a cradle and grave in one,
This place - where living begins,
And forms the growing wave
Of life's slow ebb,
Confirmed in rotting tissues.

Ah, the twilight garden!
Where God first made the human form,
And won the Devil's praise (and mine)
By cheating Adam with an apple,
And making Eve a tart.

But never let me lie
Down in God's garden grave;
However pleasantly adorned
With angels, and the like,
To bore me with their prissy messages
Of goodwill, but never, ever, goodnight!

Edwin Heath

My Shangri-La

A lovely cosy cottage
Nestles to a wooded hill
Where my fervent dreams aspire
I can my hopes fulfil
And joy has formed a happy stage,
As time itself recalls,
Immersed in mellowness of age,
Around its walls.

May you find a place like this,
Set off from worldly care,
Where you will have companionship,
And find a solace there.

Peace worldwide,
Starts first within each home.
Where friendly folk abide
And never long to roam.
In any place,
No matter where you are,
If you give tolerance, peace and love,
You will find your Shangri-La.

Patricia Edwards

JACARANDA

This should be awesome, this smell in a bottle
named for an early dusk falling on Slater Street.

Besame Mucho and Honky Tonk Angels
are tapping the shoes of a golden-ringed fat man,
kind Mr Kaye whose smile is a beacon.
Downstairs the Beatles are borrowing Rizzlas
and no-one in all of this waterlogged city,
not the bag-humping sailors,
nor the sand-raking children,
not the stilettoed cashiers
nor the vexed, queuing mothers,
not the bell-pushing busmen
nor the home-reeling fathers
care that I'm sharing the dusk with a jukebox,
three empty coffee cups,
a stuffed alligator,
that this is the very last day of my childhood.

And now I'm about to unstopper the bottle . . .

S McDermott

RICKMANSWORTH MEMORY

An uninspiring coffee shop
among a town of ordinary dreams.
Came a vision of pure excellence
that surely only I could not have seen.

Youthful, tall and slender
sunlight drenching her hair.
The way her body moved with laughter
pinned me to the chair.

Defeating, reserving weakness
I was standing close at hand.
All around was meaningless -
muttered an almost decipherable sound.

Slowing rising from her novel
two deep eyes began to sparkle.
Her eyebrows did the speaking
as that smile pursued the rascal.

Silently back to my apartment
no greater pleasure could I find.
And after our embracing glory she whispered
'Now touch the G-spot of my mind.'

Contentedly we hunger for each other
but feast at different times.
My menu is mind-boggling
while hers is easier to find.

Thoughtfulness between us
thoughtfulness in kind.
The power of stimulation
should be explored at every find.

G Winwright

PRAGUE

Necromantic city in which
Like conspirators shadows foregather
As at twilight the alchemist sun
Turns the leaden Vltava to gold

Over the tumbled graveyard
- All that is left of the ghetto -
A bat from the ivy-draped elders
Draws arabesques in the dusk

Down a dimly lit alley
Footsteps sound on the cobbles
But the doors are shut against strangers
And the windows stare out with glazed eyes

The puppet apostles strut past
As the clock in the market strikes twelve
The master who made it was blinded
To stop his constructing another

The menacing murmur of bells
Tolls for Protestant, Jesuit, Jew
The magicians were hung in iron cages
When they asked to walk out in the sun

I gazed at a carving of Christ
He stared back again with a look
That told me more than I wanted
To know how He felt on the cross.

John A Davis

Romanian Impressions

Gara de Nord, Bucuresti 1991

Passing through. Caterpillar queues at kiosks.
Jostling clamour. Bustling, spitting, smoking, shouting,
heaving bulging luggage. Lost and Found in smoky fray.

Rushing suits. Bearskin coats. Street-rags stained by sewers.
Swirling Gypsy skirts and scarves. Checked shirts. Stiff denims.
Garments oozing sweat, cheap scent, tobacco, garlic.

Steaming engine, whistle, screeching. Intermittent
blurred announcements. Touting. Swearing. Skirmish
with a knife, a chase. Arrivals and Departures.

Lei for dollars in the shadows. Woman dancing,
singing, trilling; passing out. Smashed bottles. Couples
firing words as shrill as ice. Travelling theatre.

Four Into Two Rooms: Chez Magda, Brasov 1991

Cobbled courtyard. Tapestry of vines and linen.
Roofs with squinting owl-holes. Whispers. Archways yawning.
Biting earache. Rotting cabbage. Absent birdsong.

Bathroom dank with washing; bowls of soaking jumpers,
plates, potatoes... Queue of well-scrubbed pans for Bunsen burner.
One crazed sink, one bulb. Uncurtained crowdings.

Cardboard boxes. Cupboard hoardings. Bookshelves
crammed with treasured learning. Wireless. Magda's canvas, oils.
Fresh garlic, jars of peas. Machine-gun language.

Stifling kindness. Gestures. Questions. Peering faces,
staring windows. Make-shift bed my shelter. Sickly gas
which sputters, hisses, fails to warm the chilling air.

Joanna Watson

OUTPATIENTS

Decanted from ambulance, car, taxi and bus,
In wheelchairs, on crutches, with frames or on sticks,
With plaster, foam rubber, with pain but no fuss,
Resigned to the wait.

Daddling straight for the tea bar, the clinics or loo,
In couples, or singly, with fam'ly or friend,
With children, a lover, with goodness knows who,
For moral support.

Delayed at 'Appointments', queue, with card in the hand,
'In two weeks? That's lovely' (With luck it's the last).
With light heart, recover, with hope now to stand
And wait in the rain.

J Brookes

OUR LIBRARY

Our library is a place of rest, of quiet and relaxation
With books of all descriptions that are full of information
The shelves are clearly marked so we can choose the books we need
And when they check our library card we can take them home to read.
The record on computer, gives them a forward date,
If we keep the book beyond that day a fine will be our fate,
But if we use the telephone, before the date is due
If no-one else requires the book it is easy to renew.
Now if we need a special book that they do not have around
They check computer records, for where it can be found,
And if it is available, a small fee we must pay
And then they send a dated note, 'It's available from today.'
The staff are very helpful, I know that is their task,
So if we have a query, we simply have to ask.
They have a place for children, where they can read and look
And like adults they use a card, when they take home a book.
The video we borrow, is due back the seventh day
There is also music on CD we can take away to play.
A keyboard and computer screen, is there for all to look
We can tap in all the details, to help us find a book.
A modern photocopier, is there for use by all,
With controls to change the copy size and make it large or small.
I really don't know what we'd do should libraries not exist
I am certain that for many folk, they would be sorely missed.

S F Barrett

THE CHURCHYARD

An empty church upon a hill
with its churchyard quiet and still
it stands as if a monument to religion
empty and meaningless.

Its spire does no longer thrust
upwards to where God is supposed to be
the churchyard crosses some still standing
competing with the grass in a great race to nowhere.

A bible lays with open page
a symbol of a bygone age
the hymn books shut their prayers unsung
and the bells are no longer rung
as they lay shattered as does Christianity.

Bruce Wiseman

MILLERSDALE

In the old mill at the bottom of the dale children were closely confined (working) and some died.

Come with me now to Millersdale;
Magic, mysterious Millersdale.
Wild willow herb and butterbur
Border the swiftly splashing stream;
Linger among forget-me-nots -
Follow through fragrant meadow-sweet:
Only, when the dark mill looms,
Hustle quickly by,
Before your peace may be disturbed
By a haunting childish cry.

Joyce Neville

Hampshire Winter

Lime trees, leafless now and bare
Show mistletoe in tangled hair,
The parasite that clings so high
White berries for a leaden sky.

Ivy clinging, oh so tight
Bears blossom in the weakened light,
Wrens may hide behind its curtain
Of nooks and crannies they are certain.

Winter Jasmine bold and yellow
Is a very hardy fellow,
Snow can fall and winds may blow
But in between its blooms still glow.

Primrose and yellow dandelion
In mild spells we can rely on,
So soon, snowdrop, aconite and crocus
Bloom to end our winter focus.

Denis M Pentlow

DORSET

I love my Dorset, the place I was born
The green of the meadows, the gold of the corn
There's a horse and a giant, carved in the hills high
And church towers, like fingers, that point at the sky
There's Bullbarrow Hill, and Blackmore Vale
Cranborne Chase, and Upwey Wishing Well
There's beaches of gold, and the Chesil so long
Portland so hard, Maiden Castle so strong
There's a monument to Hardy, who fought on the seas
And a statue of Hardy, who wrote the books that we read
There's towns with their markets, all full of colour
Where locals and visitors, mix with each other
I love my Dorset, and I seldom roam
But when I do, I can't wait to get home
For wherever I go, or whatever I find
Dorset still calls me, from somewhere in my mind.

E Chaffey

THE INCIDENT

Fantastic evening, missed the train.
Pitch dark night. Teeming rain.
No Taxi-cabs, no telephone.
Set off to walk, all alone.
Petrified by a desperate fear.
Stealthy footfalls, I can hear.
Panic-stricken, step up the pace.
Scalding tears, course down my face.
My vocal chords are paralysed
No-one hears, my silent cries.
Increase my speed, legs like lead.
Pain explodes inside my head.
Lungs bursting, to draw a breath
Blackest nightmare, scared to death.
Steel strong arms reach out to me
I can smell the fiend, but cannot see.
Suddenly a flashing blue light
Comes round the corner, into sight
Sobbing wildly, collapse to the ground.
No sign of assailant can be found.
Was it really my imagination.
That conjured up this vile creation.

J Fish

A Kestrel For A Knave Indeed

Oh Kestrel, Kestrel, flying high,
Hovering in the bright blue sky,
His eyes intent on prey to spy,
A thousand times they magnify,
A hundred times his wing both beat,
While waiting for a grisly treat,
A little movement on the floor,
Is all it takes to make his soar,
He hits the ground with lightning speed,
His talons close and crush with glee,
He rips and tears with wanton lust,
To fulfil a need that he must,
A ball of fur between his feet,
Is quickly turned to shredded meat,
And only when his crop is full,
Does he take flight and leave his kill,
Oh noble and majestic bird,
A knave you surely don't deserve.

J W Gummerson

SPRINGTIME

Spring is in the air
Buds of green and gold
Are appearing on the trees.
Sunlight tints the cool spring breeze,
Colours of yellow, blue and white.

Spring is in the air
Snowdrops stand like sentinels
Against the dark musky earth
Delicate white cups opening
To the warmth of the sun.

Spring is in the air
Crocus in full bloom
Such a beautiful sight
Birds sing from dawn to dusk.

Spring is in the air
Time for golden daffodils
To set their caps at the sun
While bobbing gently on the breeze.

Spring is in the air
Bringing fresh smells and colours
To scent the clear cool air
Springtime - a time for new beginnings
And a promise of summer to come.

Susan A Peach

St Mary's Lighthouse

My island - a jewel in the sea -
Charismatic, mystical, wild, free!

I am redundant now, I've had my day,
Yet I still rule the waves at Whitley Bay.

I stand tall, pristine and shining white,
Revered - a popular tourist sight.

I'm sketched, painted, photographed too,
'Neath skies of grey or brilliant blue.

I've stood the test of a hundred years,
They're as good as new - my spiral stairs.

My light has beamed across the North Sea,
Sea going men put their faith in me.

Cargo ships, fishing boats and cruisers, too.
Go sailing by with their trusty crew.

De-commissioned now, but very proud,
Never faltering in seas so loud.

There's ghost ships too, and sailors at rest -
I stand guard knowing they did their best!

For another hundred years I'll stand tall,
And still listen to the seagulls call.

My island - a jewel in the sea -
Charismatic, mystical, wild, free . . .

Pat Berkshire

THE DYING ROOM

Do not ask me what I want. You cannot give me yesterday or tomorrow or the blaze of the sun across the grass. You cannot give me what I really want. I want to own a square piece of land at the top of a mountain; as white and bare as an eyelid, as frail and as clear as bone china, on top of which I will build a perfect tomb, a small magical box, as beautiful and as tightly shut as a seashell. Just tall enough for ghosts to wander through. My own personal wound - where my dreams are kept in boxes - on this mountain.

Inside this serene vault, I want walls and walls made of tears, with blackened gold frames with mystical holy faces of saints hanging, each with a strange glassy veil - as thin as cellophane - covering them, and their pale religious faces all blue from the frosty breath of the moon; their own breath stopped long ago, sucked out from their body by hovering red dragons and sealed in small glass jars, their lungs as flat as paper inside, inside. I want eyes, eyes, eyes all over; on the ceiling, the walls, the floor.

Eyes dull and awful with no memories behind them; the death of these memories a long and lingering one, as slowly their thoughts seeped out from behind their skulls and through the paintings deep into the mortar of the walls in the guises of many thousands of white maggots. Horrific blind eyes, no answers. Eyes that merely hint at the many centuries that have been lived through. Their charred hearts are buried in me. I carry their spirits inside like a fresh organ.

I close my eyes and retreat to this - my own cold silent shrine of eyes, all held together by ribbons and your breath - whenever we fight.
I am silent but the soft whispers inside are wanting to scream out that I only want to know our souls have merged together, like our own transparent child which binds you to me; only want to know that I am not merely some spare part. I only want to know your fingers are not lying tongues and that when you look at me your thoughts are not of some other pair of eyes; which maybe shone brighter than mine in your past.

Julie Macleod

El Agheila - 1943

Here, where man is puny on this lonely stretching beach,
And sand and sea and sky in vasty panorama teach,
The loneliness of living, the inconsequence of being man . . .
Here is the terrestrial map, the omnipresent plan.

Here the abruptness of being born, and here the breath,
Foreshortened in the lusty wind that ushers death,
Faltering at the spectacle of this magnificence
Of emptiness . . . is bland Almighty reticence.

Here night sudden stills the day, and elfin light,
Unshadowed, dim, mysterious, coldly to the sight
Bears awing promise of a stiller night to come,
When all things speak, and only man is dumb.

Here, across the drifting windblown wastes of sand,
The enticing sea, close cropping on its strand,
Beckons in its deep blue green alluring voice
To such a man as might make such a spirit's choice.

Here . . . in this entity of solitude and this converging space . . .
Here, in kindly tolerance, engulfing all the race
Of man . . . here, surely, God looks down and smiles
To see *His* images steeped in such *little* wiles.

Rannoch Melville Russell

An Endless Love

I stood on the platform and kissed you once more, I heard the train coming to take you to war. We clung tight together my tears then did flow, your lips were still saying 'I do love you so.' I looked deep in your eyes and I knew just then you would never my love come back again.

The train rushed in with a mighty roar, to take you my love the one I adore. We kissed then so briefly and you waved me goodbye, the train moved forward the moment was here. Tears glistened in those eyes most dear, I shouted some words but you did not hear 'Take care my love, God be with you out there.'

The silence that followed when that train did depart, had me transfixed on that platform just the thump of my heart, my steps were heavy when I did turn away.

My eyes heavy-misted, my face drawn and grey, for I wanted to capture that moment once more. To keep forever in my heart, the face I adore, it was not to be my love.

But I relived it again, when the telegram came, I just turned away. My face tightly pressed in my hands, there was nothing to say.

Someone touched my shoulder, another my hair, someone said 'Don't cry, we are here to share.'

My grief was intense, my body had wings, my soul was in flight to entwine with yours, to stay forever with the man I adored, wrapped in the bonds of an endless love.

Sometimes I stand on that platform again, I see the train moving, a hand waves once more, I see a face smiling of the man I adore.

Vera Clarke

MIRTH ANGEL

We have an angel of the north who's
cared for institutions,
so have no need of metal chunks in need
of their ablutions.

It stands there bringing prices down of
houses in its sight,
I would not like to see it hanging
vulture-like at night.

It will have many uses for the people who
hate art,
they'll say 'don't spend your time on that
it's not worth taking part.'

Are they trying to make art a thing we need
to scrap,
or is it all for April Fools' Day and they've
set a trap.

Our angel Catherine Cookson has found lots
on which to spend,
Hospitals, education and the charitable
dividend.

Lots of people have made good from Northern
England's shores,
why not record and celebrate these instead
of choosing bores.

If we must spend a fortune on something we
don't need,
let's make it something people like, not
something they don't heed.

In marble all just black and white I'm sure they'd like to see,
A Shearer goal for England it would make more sense to me.

Jean Paisley

SEASCAPE

It came again, this spring.
. . . Walking the Graig top path.
That sea of blue
That held me like a buoy
Bobbing in its waves.

And the smell . . . Ha! The smell.
The heady aromatherapy
Made me swoon. As if in this one spot
Were all the perfumes of the world compressed.

Nowhere had I seen such depth
Of colour. It seemed that bluebells
From every corner of the globe
Were ringing out their 'Ode of Joy'
In this small glade.

And I, seeing it, as if for the first time,
In this my thirty ninth year
Of walking this glad way.

CL

On Water Leaving Great Shunner Fell

Of beauty unattainable, unharnessed - wild and free
Young, how young it is here, an innocent virgin hidden away
But later, in the distance, man will have his way
For now though there will be no blood in you.

See the dipper move in your current, and a family
of wagtails, pied - stark against your greyness
And what man could find fault?
And what woman comparative in beauty?
Could this be the first garden before sin
Before any temptress could bestride fate?

Join on be naked here
Walk proud and unchastised in here
Be at one in this sublime splendour, letting all the
infestivity wash away
Pollute the distant valley with all that is not this
Be inebriated in all she is
She is everything.

David Higgins

VIRUNGA NATIONAL PARK, ZIARE

(Where one million refugees settled)

On the Mountains of the Moon a Nile begins to flow,
travelling in snake skins to an Egypt it will know.
Natural formed unique rivers of ice and fire,
leaving hot rainforests in seclusion to perspire!
Strange majestic plants lording over the hills,
ignoring the moon and the night's misty chills.
Giant cabbages in tune appear to be on the march,
not far away sky-high peaks sit baptised in starch.
Plastered in lava icing tree soldiers stand on sentry,
tall and stark defying encroachers to make an entry!
Sharp-lipped mother hippos tending their lawns.
As decorated husbands bathe with smiles and yawns.
Sprawling before them their personal living lake,
yet nearby dirty grass where no life can partake.
Not far off gorillas on green slopes feed and play,
trying to survive in their own inquisitive way.
Thick dark shadows of mist alive with termites,
ghosting through the air with ten million bites,
for the many human souls who take refuge here
hiding away from the rancour of war with fear!
Wondering why their country is in such turmoil,
making the volcanoes angry in readiness to boil
and spew over the rivers of ice with fire again.
Deadly! Upsetting the balance of forest and rain!

K F Adamson

BAD MEMORIES

He won't visit the town
in which he lived
for six years because
of too many bad memories.

He does have good memories
of living there,
but within the clenched fist
of bad memories
the good memories are entombed.

He possesses the strength
to pry open the fingers
from the clenched fist
so that the good memories
are seen and remembered,
but he won't.

He needs bad memories
so that the actions
which created them
won't be repeated.
Bad memories
are the forefathers
of his good memories.

David Rhine

Look, Stranger!

I climb the steps, and see the tower rise.
Gargoyles gaze down where silent faithful lie.
I place my hand upon the ancient door
and wonder whether treasures wait within -
of angels bright or poppy heads or screen;
of painted wall or table centuries old?

No need to know some arcane, magic word -
Open, sesame! Abracadabra!
The door swings open. History lies bare.
Silent, I step inside this sacred space
where wonders wait, and 'prayer has been valid'.

I spy in brick-laid nave, a modest brass
lovingly polished, a memorial
to Rose of Charsfield (Parson Glover's wife),
who died December 1620. I kneel
to read the quaint old-English elegy.

'As wither'd Rofe its fragrant fent retains
So beinge dead, her vertue ftill remains
shee is not dead, but chang'd. Y[E] *good ne'er dies*
But rather shee, is Sun=like, fett to rife.'

A simple plaque, naturally adorned with
stylised Tudor rose - and humble daisy!
Its older name, 'day's eye', the secret holds.
Sun sets, sleep comes, and pinky lashes close
but, with the morning bright, 'day's eyes' awake,
expanding petals to God's glorious light.

The rose and daisy spoke to me
in *selig* Suffolk's silence, though
about four hundred years had passed
since their first flowering.

Doreen McPherson

Up-River

Deep the sea - unfathomed and deep
below strong waves that never sleep,
between some rocks, a spiralled shell
a sea-carven house where a hermit crab dwells.

Fish swim up-river, freshwater to seek
a cormorant, diving takes one in his beak.
Salmon splash up from the broad water mouth
joining with swallows, returned from the south.

A pair of wild ducks shooting out of the sky
down to the river they noisily fly
dodging an oar of a fisherman's boat
cocking an eye at the bright bobbing float.

A family of swans, sail by some tall reeds
where birds of the riverbank quietly feed,
moorhens and coots, there, have hidden their nests
and anxiously watch lest a thief steal an egg.

And so the river winds slowly inland
to a trickling brook where the journey began
a bright crystal spring is the river's new birth
bubbling gently, up, out of the earth.

Alan Cole

Treescape In Provence: Perpetuum Mobile

The trees I see are yellower this year.
They work such magic in the failing sun:
My breath runs wild each time I turn my head,
Shocked into wonder at the moving glow.
Whenever silence reigns, whenever light,
Then I'm a prisoner, then I am soothed.

My mind runs barefoot through the countryside,
It flies alone through sunshine, over crag,
It fills its lungs with hidden space and joy,
Cooling itself with green of branch and grove,
But while my mind so races, I must stay:
The moment of fulfilment has not come.

In quieter moments, too, the trees will speak.
The terrace fills with ghosts and memories
Which stare from vine and climbing ivy leaves.
The branches tremble, echoing the past,
While homeland urges, calling strongly back.

The massive pines twist violently and strain
Beneath the frenzied mistral's husky fire.
Delirious branches circle, gleaming gold,
And tease the sunlight in their savage play.
The dance excites me too, and I would race
To rave with them, till my impatience dies.
But no, not yet, it is not yet the time.

Descend the wooded hill, the cliffs, the beach.
The early evening sun still lights the peaks,
And breaking water foams round jagged rocks.
Yet now I cannot pause and, wondering, stand.
The quiet and the rugged beauty fail:
I must walk on; I cannot stop and think . . .

Anne Sanderson

Sense Of Place

She is alive with the evidence of many things,
Sunbeams,
Rainbows,
Fruit,
Flowers,
Dripping water,
Brooks and streams,
And between the happy castles of her tiny breasts
The place of all my dreams.

She is alive with the evidence of many things,
Laughter,
Happiness,
Goodness,
Joy,
Ecstasy proclaiming its existence to the wind,
Worthiness and fire,
And between the near-perfect fold of her limbs
The sense of all desire.

George Jeffery

A Wessex Hill

Wessex in the twilight hour,
A barrow on a windblown rise,
Where ghostly grey-barked beeches tower,
Their branches traced against the skies.
Soft grasses clothe the ancient mound
With silver seed heads gently blown.
Kings' secrets hidden underground,
Buried heroes, lives unknown.

But sometimes when the windsong slows,
A timeless silence draws aside
The veil of ages in repose,
Chronology itself untied.
And across the modern hillsides sigh
The faintest ring of warring blades.
A distant, muffled battle cry
That mocks the ear, then swirls and fades.

And through the falling shades of night
Beyond the stately columns grey,
Is that a campfire's orange light
Or just the dying of the day?
And are those sounds, so faintly heard,
That taunt and tease your straining ear,
The roosting chatter of a bird
Or voices from a bygone year?

But as the shadows melt and flow,
And darkness robs the eye of sight,
The timeless earth alone can know
The secrets of that mystic height.

J C Turner

THE OLD HOUSE

The old house stood in acres of land
Surrounded by a fantastic view
Climbing ivy ascending the walls
Glistening with dew.

The oaks and elms which stood so tall
Cast their shadows around
Landscaped garden and shrubbery
And stepping-stones set in the ground

The house and land was picturesque
Just like an old oil painting
With its atmosphere of serenity
I imagined a lady-in-waiting.

I stood aside absorbing the scene
And breathing in the air
I closed my eyes momentarily
And wished that I lived there.

C Giles

The Joys Within My Garden

The joys within my garden are there for all to see,
And they are very meaningful, especially to me.

The Roman arch majestically it stands against the sky,
A landmark grey which can be viewed by all who pass it by.

Upon a plinth below it a bust of bronze now stands,
In thoughtful pose, with eyes cast down on ivy-clinging bands.

A mask of Amphitrite, it rests upon a base,
Near her husband Neptune with heavily-bearded face.

The verdant branches of the trees aloft the windswept wall,
Give welcome shelter to some birds when scattered showers fall.

The statuary and cultured plants are mingling side by side,
And several colourful blossoms spread their fragrance far and wide.

The trickle of the fountain and the chirping of each bird
Give a really soothing feeling when by listeners they are heard.

Within my rustic sanctuary, a cosy, wood-clad nook,
I paint and draw or write and sew or read a favourite book.

Here I'm in another world when nature's fruits abound
On luscious branches overhead or sprouting from the ground.

To God I give my thanks for the wonders that I see
Within this classic garden which means so much to me.

Yvonne Watkin-Rees

Born By The Wash

When a tiny child, with Dad's hand to hold,
The sea was so rough, but I felt so bold,
As we walked along by the edge of the sea,
I loved the feeling of being free,
All sorts of rubbish was left on the shore,
Where had it been before?

With childish innocence I watched the waves,
Thought of the big ships driven by slaves,
So many lands were over this sea,
I wondered, would a ship one day come and take me?
Each time Dad and I walked on the shore
I dreamed more and more.

Returning home to a warm welcome drink,
I would sit, face aglow and quietly think,
No words could describe my childish dreams,
Now that I'm old unfulfilled dreams, it seems,
I'd love one day to walk again on that shore,
Just once more.

Fleur Lusher

PRECIOUS TIME

A moonlit night still
Silent clouds drift along
A darkened sky

Chilling breeze broken by
Sheltered nest warm and snug
In nature's surroundings

Wriggling tangled movement
Exchange feelings of comfort
And much joy

Silhouette shadow, graceful
Wings in flight lighten
From silver beam

Times pace slow unfolding
Rest from life
Before reality returns.

Ivan George Barber

CORNWALL

Oh rugged rugged coastline,
How the light on you does shine.
Wherever I may roam,
You will always be my home.

Oh rugged rugged coastline,
You're always in this heart of mine.
Although the sea is wide,
And he is by my side.

Oh rugged rugged coastline,
As we sailed I began to pine.
How long before I see
And along your paths walk free.

Oh rugged rugged coastline,
One day all will be fine.
I will answer your magic call,
My wonderful love, Cornwall.

J Guy

A VIEW

I remember a view
Seen as a child
Somewhere on pillar
The weather was mild
I'm sure we descended
Down an anonymous ghyll
Where tranquil blue water
Left time standing still
The mist it then covered
All to the fore
My view disappeared
And left my heart sore
I hope every day
My place I can find
And pray it is not
Just a part of my mind.

Mike Naylor

My Bath

I like to take an evening bath,
And leave my cares behind.
The water flows around me,
All stress goes from my mind,

I close my eyes and daydream,
Indulge in fantasy
I'm in the Caribbean,
On a ship out in the sea.

I lay on sands that glisten,
The sun is beating down.
Basking my white body,
To a lovely golden brown.

I beckon to the waiter,
Who pours an ice-cold beer.
He rubs in suntan lotion,
And whispers in my ear.

A hunky man approaches,
And drops down on one knee.
Other women on the beach,
Just look on enviously

He takes me to his villa,
And plies me with champagne.
He lays me gently on the bed,
And kisses me again.

By now I'm just past caring,
I'm feeling really bold.
But that's all I can tell you,
'Cause my water's getting cold.

Tina Smith

Evening At St Brelade's Bay

Waves, blush red
'Neath setting sun
Advance shyly
Towards the waiting sand,
Whispering, enticing.

Waves recede,
Now bolder, return
To caress the softness
With coaxing,
Exploring fingers.

Waves urgently
Advance and retire,
Advance and rear up
To consume
The willing captive.

Rosaline Pilley

The Urban Knight

Sitting staring at the lake below.
Perched on a rock in this high place
I daydream about a green dragon
He stands blowing fire from his nostrils
Perhaps a beautiful princess is
Cowering in that cave nearby.
I draw a breath of the ice-cold air,
Now I am a knight of old in shining armour.
I imagine the battle
The dark rocks echoing as we fight it out,
Then the dragon is gone
And in the distance a train clatters along
Bringing the dream to a close
Goodbye princess, I shall return on the morrow.

Tim Warren

The Mountain

Caressed in moonlight proud and tall
The mountain loomed, surveying all
Dark, mysterious, silent, cold
Chilling fingers gnarled and old

Whispering shadows filled the night
Souls in torment taking flight
Ghosts of travellers, victims all
Succumbed to her magnetic call

Eerie in the soft veiled light
Moonlight treads her pathways trite
A mantle worn with snowy sleeves
And pearls of mist exquisite please

Soft sweet silver light of moon
A fantasy within the gloom
As playfully in feathery flakes
And icicled in unformed shapes

The twilight of all Gothic things
The scent of briar, owls on wing
The mountain fills my heart and soul
Her untamed beauty beckons, calls

Caressed in moonlight, wild and free
This haunting place screams out for me
To walk and climb, release my chains
The fervour pitching in my veins

Darkening storm clouds frame the moon
The whistling wind to lace the flume
Her wild and sensuous beauty fills
My thoughts, my eyes, my heart, my will

Bathed in sunshine all her charms
No warning thoughts to sound alarms
The mysteries of this mountain high
Are lost when robed in azure sky.

Susie Barker

Colours In Tunisia

The dusty grey-green olive tree
Spreads up the hill and sings to me
Of ancient plots and ancient ways
Punic, Roman, Berber days.

Soft shadow-green cypress sentinel stands
Halts swooping winds across the land
And when the midday break is made
Workers rest in spice-smell shade.

Shouting from the crowded Souk
Are lovely pots in white and blue
Deep purple-blue contrast to white
Dazzles in the sun-washed light.

Spices gold, orange, yellow, red,
Colours swirl inside my head
Soft powdered pyramids of taste
Pungent smells the rich air grace.

Ancient is the carpet art
Its colours reach straight to my heart
Blood-red, deep pink, soft powder blue
A rainbow shower of every hue.

And in that time my eye-brain filled
All shades from painters' palettes spilled.
A head full of pictures, a nose full of smells
Enchanted by this sun-swept spell
Returning to my pale north strand
Drunk with the colours of this land.

Charmian Goldwyn

NORTHERN DELIGHTS

Surrounded by mountains
Some capped with snow
Still wearing my T-shirt
In the valley below
Subject to adversities
Is the northern weather
But nothing as consistent
As the scent of the heather
The tame rabbits hop
The roe deer go by
The red squirrels play
The ospreys soar high
The river runs wild
The salmon leap
The sheep dog looks tired
As he gathers the sheep
The fisherman wades
He casts out his fly
Oblivious of time
As it rushes him by
The air is now crisp
The sun lowering down
Underfoot is carpeted
With leaves golden brown
The sun is now swallowed
By the high mountain peaks
A crisp autumn day
Now turns so bleak.

Iain Barr

I Knew That You Were There

I felt your presence Lord in the gentle breeze,
As it gently swayed the lush green grass,
I knew that you were there,
It seemed to whisper my child I love you and I care.

I felt your presence Lord in the golden sun,
that makes things grow and warms the children as they play,
I knew that you were there,
It seemed to say my child let me have my way.

I felt your presence Lord in the vast blue sky
that reaches further than the eye can see
like a great curtain over me,
It spoke so quietly to my heart, my child give me every part.

I felt your presence Lord in the cool refreshing rain
that waters all the earth and makes things grow again,
It seemed to say to me, my child I want to set you free.

I felt your presence Lord in the rolling sea,
as it cleans the golden sand and washes over me,
It whispered gently to my soul, my child I want to make you whole.

I felt your presence Lord in my tears as they did flow,
I thought my heart would surely break you said my child I know,
I see your sad and tear-stained face, I feel your aching heart,
give your burdens all to me I want to be a part.

I felt your presence Lord as I came to Calvary and
I thought about the cross and the death you died for me,
and I told you all my guilty sin and asked you to forgive,
then you welcomed me with open arms and said, yes my child you live.

I feel your presence Lord because it's everywhere,
whether we are happy or deep down in despair,
you're always there with open arms calling us to you,
wherever we are or whatever we do.

So thank you for your presence Lord as I fall down to my knees,
and I think about the wonder of your sun and sky and breeze,
and of all that you've created, and all the things you do,
But most of all Lord, the wonder of you.

Antoni Strich

LECTURE OF ROSES AND HEARTHS

A busy night
for one now used to solitude.

Alone,
she sits among a crowd
of enthusiastic Saturday night oldies,
desperate to catch an education
(more likely to catch a cold),
who fidget in seats made for smaller bottoms
and proffer polite attention
as if they are being offered
a meal which is not to their liking.

Amazing how engrossed
she can appear in unrefined words
from the evening's anonymous speaker
when all she wants to do is cut
out his man's tongue
for the love he devotes
to all things Rennie Mackintosh
and missing roses,
but not her.

Through his words
she burns at the injustice
which has brought her to this cold place
and shown her a warmth
absent, by default,
from her own hearth.

J Alex Guthrie

Ghost Town

The Turkish people feel such guilt,
For the township the Greeks once built,
Shipped out never to return to their home
The buildings stand forlorn and alone
As you walk through the ruins in the heat of the day
The silence alone seems to say 'stay away'
As you walk along the once cobbled pathways
Peer through windows which are now just dark holes,
You feel and sense the people and their lost souls
Nobody lives there, it's like a giant tomb, broken
Down but not forgotten as tourists walk by,
Your skin feels prickly but not from the heat of the
Blue sky, or the rays of the sun
But thinking with sadness of people long gone
Never to return again not a single one.

Patricia Widdowson

CAERPHILLY MOUNTAIN

The rugged pathway seamed with gold,
Parallel beams, heavens unfold,
Parchment sky blue fingerprints there,
Caerphilly Mountain's landscape rare.

Bird's eye view distant sea,
Flat and steep holms bask,
Balmy breeze a violin tease,
Stringed kites held fast.

Laughter, family picnics shared,
Habitat wild and free, nature's scents,
Misty hues, vision to eternity,
Passageway treacherous, illuminations at night.

Wealth of dawn, remnant torn,
Tourist in awe delight,
Steaming forests, silent hills,
Golden host of daffodils.

Castle, history, culture strong,
Choirs echoing church bells toll,
Wales forever! Land of song.

Eileen Brown

SNAKE

A snake, eyes opaque,
skin dry and husky
light brown and rusty,
slithered from his hole
and curdled my soul.
His tongue flicked well
tasting my smell,
he curled round a rock
ignoring my shock.
Then, snake split his skin
as from deep within
shone riotous colour
as bright as a flower
a symphony in brown
adorning the ground.
The pair of us lay
skin touching that day.
I studied he and
he studied me
while together we basked in the sun.
Then the big puff adder
in harlequin hues
slithered his length
down my leg cross my shoe,
I wished death well
as he vanished from view
that powerful day in the mountains
of Malawi.

Hamish Lee

SCOTLAND

Mountains reach from rugged hill,
Reach to claim the sky.
Look up on brooding beauty,
Upon Scotland and give sigh.
See lands clothed and warmed in brackened golds,
(That cushioned the fall of those history now holds)
Let gaze fall upon deep-purpled heather,
That endures against time and the sternest, cruel weather.
See hill upon hill enfold cosseted glen
As mists enfold mountain, come ye, rest th'sen,
In a land steeped in spirited . . . bloody a past,
Spells on each sassenach heart are here cast.
Those mists but the cloak of angel wings
While, in homage to the clans, remembrance brings.
Those lost to the future, to live on in memory
Are sung of in pride, no longer as enemy.
The lochs and the glens yet hold to their story
Of clan peoples gone, but only to glory.
Tartan-true colours in splendour march yet,
The silence shouts of its heritage - lest any forget.

V G Walker

DESERTED

I lie on the long, endless plains
Of my bed.

My tall, imposing physique
Seems sadly slight and enfeebled.
I fling my limbs outward
Like a child learning to float,
Attempting to prove that I'm self-sufficient;
Yet, child-like, I can't fill the pool.
Underneath my duvet heavens
The darkness sidles in
Dredging my body of warmth;
And happiness.
The single solitary pyre of my heart
Will stay colourless and silent tonight.
There is no provoking spark.
Even the pillow won't yield
To my orders; evading pitiful
Claspings and graspings;
Circling my head like
A sarcastic vulture.
Smothering's out of the question.

The sun will rise, of course.
Day will set in with all
The usual busy accoutrements.
I will be thawed into a
Semblance of control.

It's a long time until morning.

Gareth Lewis-Jones

The Ghost City

We stood at the lookout. Through glasses provided
We could see the rough lines where the land was divided
Directly ahead no-man's land was in view
And further to left we saw NATO flags flew
Still further flew flags of a different nation.
Very peaceful it seemed, yet we had the sensation
That big unseen guns pointed in our direction
Would spew forth without mercy at any defection
By those, or by one, who might break through the lines
To get to the city which lay further behind,
Where tall buildings loom, where although windows shine
No one lives or works there, and the silence gives truth
That there is no industry; still further proof
Is provided by cars left abandoned in haste
By those who sought freedom. It all seems a waste.
And when I remember that visit that day
I am filled with a sadness that won't go away
Then I think of the innocent people who grieve
For those taken hostage for what they believe.
And the lonely ghost city convinces me more
That the thing we should fight for is end to all war.

Dianne J Shorthouse

Crete

Silent majesty of mammoth mountains
Cicadas chirping in cypress groves
Basking in sun and sweet salt sea
Sleeping wrapped in a blanket
On stony ground
Beneath bright stars
Free.
Olives and ouzo
Learning, yearning, journeying
Moods sway throughout the day
Nostalgic ponderings
Meandering philosophies
Underwater yoga
Underlying logic of magic
Drumbeat whiteheat
Jangling goat bells
See?

Emma Fordham

PANACEA FOR SLEEPLESSNESS

Many white woolly clouds have sailed over gates
I've fatigued my brain with repetitive dates
Still I'm wearily wide awake.

'Imagine your arms and legs are numb,
And you doze and dream by the sea in the sun.
Be calm,' I tell myself.

Lazily curling and looping through *calm*
Evokes flowing waves and green ozonic balm
Spray on my face salts the tip of my tongue.

Warm sinking sand snugly cradles around me
Sun's heat weighs on my eyelids so heavily
I won't lift them.

I can swim in the depths of the navy-green swell,
Track the cool, fizzy edge of the white bubble trail
or linger and sleep . . .

Felicity M Bradley

My Garden

When springtime comes
And the days grow warm,
there's a place I love to be,
Away from the hustle, bustle and noise
It's a heaven on Earth to me
There the blackbird sings
And the magpies perch
In the shade of a sycamore tree,
There the clematis makes
A curtain of pink
Forget-me-nots a carpet of blue
Heathers and lavenders abound
In every shade and hue
Sometimes a squirrel comes
In from the woods
To search for a nut or two.

When evening comes
And the shadows fall
It's a haven on Earth so dear
And I seem to hear the Lord Jesus say
'Be still, for I am here,'
So I thank the Lord
For this garden of mine,
As I tend it with loving care
For this garden of mine
Is a lovesome thing
And to me beyond compare.

Olive Eves

A Field Asleep

Through furrows etched in silver,
Wearily, trod he,
Far beyond the blacksmith's glen,
Through the sleepy murmurs of Wayland fen,
Through the corn furrows yet to be.

Where once the autumn ears danced,
Golden, upon the wave,
Now beneath a winter's star sprawled shroud
Strode he without a cloud
To mar the glow the moon gave.

Summer's fallen fruit, about,
Through seasons to earth anchored,
Once immersed in shadow, glistened,
While he who traversed in dream time listened;
Was greeted by naught, for naught laboured.

About him, the ghost field swayed;
Silent sweeps of corn;
Dark wintry furrows
Above labyrinthine burrows,
Yet in the summer tide to be born.

Onward to sweet harvest, he sighed,
When thriving, he thought, this field
Will dance beneath a sun drenched land,
Not sleep beneath starry winter's hand,
And the ragged hawthorns will the moon yield.

Sean Rooney

Kasbah

Slabbed, dust-strewn flaggings floor the sandlings
Of this sun-worn vale.
White houses, baked in sunlight, trap their noonday shades
In shadowed shale.
Ancient, plodding highway.
Time-encrusted stone.

Shawls, bags and bracelets hang like offerings
From the cluttered stalls.
And smoke-grained faces light up in the raucous strain
Of haggling calls.
Leather: warm and fragrant.
Strange tongues all around.

Small, grimy children trail the sippers
Of the mint-green wells.
The charmer coils the cobra, while the carrier chinks
His watery bells.
Camel-scented doorways.
Vacuumed, desert air.

Alison Dugmore

SENSE OF PLACE

From my solitary position I can see it all.
My nose imprisons the fragments of salt in the air.
My eyes fall on the distant landscape adorning the horizon.
I can hear the angry waves beating against the innocent pebbles.
Punishing them with its passionate blows.
Virginal white joined with abundant blues.
Then my feet fall on the golden grains.
I am now touched by the magical water.
Your eyes attract your soul
- Suddenly you want to jump in.
The freedom.
Rippling water deciding your destiny - your head a buoy
Fantasy?
My hand falls on a shrunken rock and I propel it into the sea.
The larger rocks lay beneath the mirror of blue.
You cannot lie to the sea - it always gives a true picture.
The water meets my feet and edges closer to its home.
It will be gone again by morning but will always return.

Emma Cottell

My Meadow

The sun kisses the flowers all sparkling with dew
Lifting their heads as the doves start to coo.
A rabbit peeps out and looks all around
Apart from the bird song there isn't a sound.
A butterfly lands on a flower with grace
If I had my way I would stay in this place.
And if I could see heaven I know it would be
Just as peaceful and quiet as this place I see.

Evelyn Ingram

Sweet Sorrow

When the flowers of the Daphne
Sweetly scent the moonlit air,
It's time to hark, be still,
To listen for you there.

Across the frosty darkness
Of a clear sapphire night,
Your delicate, brittle purity
Is a joyful heart's delight.

A lonely, lifting sound,
A cosy, haunting tune,
A joyful, woeful melody
That is over all too soon.

And so you find another
And then you're quickly gone,
As I remain to listen in vain
For the beautiful nightingale's song.

But oh! To take such music
For a treasure is my goal,
To set some free on rainy days
To radiate my soul!

Andrea Noelle Vaughan

A Shopping Centre

There is a kind of peace around
Of love and beauty that abound,
From people passing in the street
With moving purpose for busy feet.
Their footsteps are like buzzing bees
Move, like a dance all round me.
Sitting here, people passing
Doing all their daily shopping.

Wars may come and wars may go
But in the street all to'ing and fro'ing
Comes from the toil of daily shopping.
Something for tea and something for super
Maybe a bill or maybe a cuppa.
And through this mass of walking shoe,
Dogs are seen and pigeons coo,
Prams are swapped for baby trollies
No signs of crying but plenty of lollies.

Music, heard within the beat
Young girls and boys out in the street,
Not buying, but spying, on one another
Maybe a sister, or maybe a lover!
And food is sometimes thrown for me
This is a bird's-eye view you see.

Lynda Hughes

SUNSET

The lap of thewaves, the blueness of the sky, the sunset that followed our meeting, a short space in time was given to us, our conversation seemed fleeting.
Two kindred spirits, that thought as one, in tune with nature and art, I saw in you a part of me, that circumstance kept apart.
I skimmed stones across the water, oblivious to your gaze, you lay on the sand with book in hand, and spoke of former days.
Of a childhood spent in this coastal town, and happy teenage years, then learning called and London town and performing arts careers.
You said you loved the sunset, disappearing behind the sea, we could be in the Caribbean you said, with a little imagery.
To speak with you, opened my mind, and things became more clear, just what I had been looking for, was now before me here.
We watched the sun go down together, to acknowledge the stars' arrival, I said to her 'What is that book?' 'It is my Holy Bible.'
We smiled a smile, and said goodbye, our conversation done, not only was she a true Christian girl, but a soulful and talented one.

A S McKay

TWO FACES OF GOA

The almost empty sands at dawn.
The sun just hazing in the sky.
The scuttling sand crabs running free.
And fishing boats arriving by.

Small sandpipers face the sun
In droves, so silent and so still.
And not so far two dolphins leap,
As splashing waves my senses fill.

The day moves on and the sun beats down.
It would be too hot without the breeze.
The sellers start to amble round
Arms loaded with their silken wares.

With silver bangles on their arms,
Or fruit piled high on stately heads,
Their smiles and pleas one can't resist
For bartered items to fill my case.

But then I take the Margao road
To that busy, dusty Goan town.
With dirty streets and broken paves,
And barefoot people all around.

The smell of fish and curry mingle,
And wide-eyed children play and jostle
Among the bikes and scooters, buses, beggars,
Barrows, payphones, cashew nut sellers.

The market like an oven wafting
Smells of spices and scented flowers.
But o I love it, heat and people
To remember in my dreamy hours.

Brenda H Bradbury

CALIFORNIA AGAIN

Back in California
I am trying to find my feet again,
to find my words.

This old barn sings with bees
and bees I know,
I remember an English hedge
alive with humming.

This ground has been farmed
and farms I know
from walking through
the English picture-book fields
past munching sheep
on wet evenings.

Then there is the forest
and forests I know
though not so wild and mountainous as this.

And there are people and people I know
in small places like this
where the shared space brings community.

From the days of the Indians onward
so many feet have walked this place
to leave their imprint on the earth.
And there were hands that worked
And planted trees.

So my feet too, as they walk this land,
send messages to my hands, my mind,
to help me find my place again.
My words will follow.

Pam Redmond

Walking Back To Durdle-Door

Coming back form Lulworth Cove
To the friendly hills of Durdle-Door
Walking along the shimmering road
Hot from the afternoon sun

Cows in the field beside me
One runs fast to the black fence
Flicking her tail, up, round, down, over
Flick, flicking the flies away

Butterflies hover low fluttering
Along the verge, the random wind
Bending wild and scrawny leafy grasses
Mingled with dandelions and cups of blue

A meadow over the way displays
Narrow carpets of yellow flowers
And some in bunches stand
Like a picture without a frame

Gypsy wild wind, blowing through my hair
Along the pave-less road
Brings the earth's core to my skin
And blends as one like milk and honey

Walking the road back to Durdle-Door
The living breathing Dorset hills
Where nature brings excitement
Treading lightly, in the summer sun.

Gladys Llewellyn

BUSSING IT

The sun comes up like a bloody great orange
Silvery jet-trails zip up the sky
As if such pale fragility might fall apart, or try

Every inanimate object is sugared with frost
Except where feet have trodden, hands have brushed, or wheels criss-crossed.

At every stop, a huddle of cold humanity, fidgeting, stamping, breathing hot vapours of impatience, like fettered horses, eager to be gone.

Each one boards with tangible relief
Red noses, watered eyes, fumbling for change with cold fingers
while those behind refrain from rushing on.

The mood is lighter now in such brief solace
A little warmth, a seat, some friendly chat
'Hello, how are you?' 'Ain't it cold?' 'This blooming bus is always bloody late!'

The sun is higher now, more like a coppered disc.
The frost's receding wetly in the shine
The bus fills up as journey's end approaches
From end to end, those standing form a line.

The mood is not so jovial now, we find
as bodies like sardines begin to grind
upon each other's nerves, as the bus jolts and swerves
Sheer weight of numbers makes it such a bind.

And I have got to get off next, I frown
long before we reach the favoured town
Through throngs of irate bodies I must fight
before I can in confidence alight.

But when I finally make it, I am free
The clear, cold morning seems to welcome me
Alone, unfettered - what a treat it seems
Ten minutes I must walk with just my dreams

And no more buses till the evening stint . . .

Bernadette Morris

UNTITLED

I left Dalry some time ago
To go to work on farms.
It was what I wanted.
It was the life for me.
I never got a wife;
I got a little friend.
She meant the world to me
We worked together for five years
On and off the farms.
She took ill at Christmas time
In nineteen ninety seven
I took her to the vet's,
To see what they could do.
They treated her with kindness;
They treated her with love.
They did their best for my little Tess.

You ask me how I feel;
I feel alone and empty;
I feel it in my heart.
I am sorry what has happened
I know it's for the best.
I am going away to face a job
And it is scaring me.
She rests upon a hill,
A place like where she was born.
She will always be with me.
Her memory will never die.

Iain A Murray

WATERSCAPE

Sheep, with Roman noses, shuffle grass
munching mud flat land. Fields of frogs
chunk lozenge shapes across the marsh.
Churches squat like hunchbacks
sodden underneath
a sky swallowing waterscape
washed in mist.

Dymchurch every year.
Two weeks digging in the sand
buckets gritted full of shells
starfish dried to a draining pink
lug worm casts in filtered squiggles
scuttled crabs and rock pool shrimps
squeamishing eye-level swim
of jellyfish.

To Saltwood Castle Becket's knights
crept in disconsolate shame.
In Hythe the crypt is stacked in skulls
chill fragments of some plague.

Scoured by sea at Dungeness
the fog bites back through slats and pots.
A magpie collared lighthouse.
Pylon stalking moon.

My ghosts of Romney Marsh.
Filigree instant of recall,
a cobweb twisting yet.

Mandy Pannett

THE SCENT OF THE LILIES

I can smell all my life from these things -
Fresh mint a reminder of new potatoes and summer days,
The pungent odour of some brown irises I once grew,
Attar of roses, a whiff of June -
A bowl of pot-pourri,
Beyond all this, the scent of the lilies.

Sandra Lewis

Cardiff Bay

Waters had slowly crept from the bay,
A variety of boats in random array,
Disused dry docks, gates breaking down,
Thick mud in the bottom, glutinous grey brown,
A myriad of footprints tracking to and fro,
Seagulls searching now the tide is so low,
Down dry dock walls, ladders hang askew,
No more a descent for shipyard crews,
A mewing overhead as a seagull calls,
Scanning for food along now empty walls
Where once had been a thriving port,
Now was forming a tourists' resort.
A single track railway ran to the bay
A pleasant place to while a few hours away
To take in a museum or a waterfront stroll,
Harry Ramsden's if hunger takes its toll.
Clank of steel at new buildings being built,
Clank of steel on a dredger dredging silt,
Quiet of evening, reflections of light,
Moon-beamed waters illuminating the night.

Ray Lewis

Newark-On-Trent

Wise the old steeple, vigilant the clock,
As they look down on cobbled market square
And seem to say to all the passers-by
Let they anachronism build who dare.
So tastefully, functional modern cubes
And all the trappings of our present ways
Are hidden or blend imperceptibly
With grand reminders of the olden days.
Walk where you may, the little lanes and gates
Courtyards, arcades and alleys all beguile,
The centuries compressed in brick and stone,
More snug by far than urban High Street's mile.
For therein lies the charm of Newark town,
The cosy compact squareness of the place
That seems to show for me the very best
Ideal of quiet dignity and grace.
And tho' the ancient castle looks to brood
O'er the imponderable Trent below,
How friendly and how welcoming its walls
Resplendent in the sunset's golden glow.

D Mitchell

VILLAGES OF MYSTERY

Villages of mystery,
Seen across a rolling landscape,
Not visited and unknown,
Except by the image,
Washed clean by distance,
And presented to the traveller,
On the road, two miles away.
What are the dark brown shapes of walls,
And deep blue roofs of slate really like?
What sort of people live there?
Folk at distance look very much the same,
Lovely or ugly; all blend into one,
To a man standing far enough away.

Is there dry rot in those roofs,
Wet rot in the floors,
Water with frogs and slugs in cellars?
Are there architectural gems of style,
Precious things centuries old,
Deserving preservation,
Yet sagging into decay?
People in crowds,
Are like villages seen far off,
Beneath the fashion and the style,
Under the concocted youth preserved,
The unseeing arrogant aloofness,
Which marks the heaving crowd,
What are the picture people really like?

Roger Hodges

AT WATERGATE BAY

Granite prows
Confront the sea.
Ochred the rocks,
Flecked with emerald,
Slaty, with secret caves.

Waves advance and retreat,
Gathering, filling the pools,
Frothing over sleek sand.

Skies heavy. Tears of rain.
Gulls' plangent cries,
Wings lifting and beating.

Swiftly, before the wind,
Time bears this moment away.

Irene Snatt

Rest By The Riverside

Tree tops swaying in the breeze,
River slowly gliding by,
Walkers ambling at their ease,
Hills and farmland all are nigh.

Moorhens, ducks and swans swim past.
Hoping to be fed each day,
Children soon appear with crust,
Food in plenty comes their way.

Looking from this sunlit bower,
Ancient buildings one espies,
Guildhall, town hall, deanery tower,
Church spire rising to the skies.

Sitting in this place of peace,
Close beside an ancient town,
One can contemplate the race,
Modern man has made his own.

Is this truly how to live,
Should we not find time to stare?
Time and care to others give,
Peace and quiet, now so rare.

All the beauty which surrounds,
In a place so quiet as this,
Makes one's heart with joy abound,
Fills one with a sense of bliss.

Ruby Ling

TRAIN FROM LONDON

Your thighs encased in dark, blue tights
where your skirt rode higher as you crossed your legs
and calmly contemplated your
apple, your
pain in the neck.

Chewing on the green bites within
your pink pillowed mouth.

You pulled your skirt down
and released me
checked the position of your boots
and smoothed your straightened hair.

The long grey gloves came off,
then on, rearranged, you picked at the
apple skin with your tongue,
between your teeth.

Got up and left.

Helen Pisarska

On Call

The moon shines through the broken cloud,
and dimly lights the scene.
Of the tomcat sat upon the wall,
with eyes of emerald green.

His eyes look round at the rising tower,
where the practise rescue's made.
And in the corner an old hose lies,
with all its webbing frayed.

The cat gracefully lands in the station yard,
still wet from the previous day.
But an echo of laughter is all that is left,
of the jokes from the men at play.

The engines stand unearthly still,
as the cat walks past them all.
But the doors are open, they're always prepared,
for any emergency call.

Upstairs the men are dreaming dreams,
of fires they've fought and won.
And of risks they've taken to save a life,
all part of a job well done.

The cat walks back across the yard,
and jumps up at the wall.
While the moon shines through the broken cloud,
at the station below 'on call.'

Jacquie Dimmer

Sea Ghosts

At dusk along the white fragmented shore
When wind has stripped all beauty from the sea
Where laughter's surging echoes long have ceased
And yellow fingers patch the soundless quay.
There from summer's end till waves are bent
And breezes slough the sunlit earth to dust
Lost fragments of ourselves, moon-born,
Live on our secret longing as they must.

All merging they are spread, on sand now cold
Search there for all the pleasures now so still
In perfect bays drenched with a thousand ghosts
Whose edgeless shapes can only partly fill
They pass unseen, save where one ancient star
In patient orbit of the evening sky
Looks down as those pale shadows drift
And round the headlands of our dreaming fly.

W E Hobson

Sunset In Provence

On such a night as this,
A southern night,
All seems at peace,
All tension smoothed away.

The sun behind the Brouis
Has hid his light
And sinks to ease
The passing of the day.

Above the sepia hills
The lambent sky
Shines like a lamp
And incandescent glows;

And slowly colour spills.
It spreads like dye -
A parting stamp
Of amethyst and rose.

In lemon, gold and jade
The pigments flow
Between the sky
And far horizon's bar.

Now, as the bright hues fade
To indigo,
The moon sails high
Towing the shepherd's star.

Evelyn Westwood

Paws For Thought

Artist on pavement
The crowd passing by
Body recumbent
The chalk to apply.

Holding stick lightly
He colours the ground
Beside him quietly
Lies his trusty hound
Conscientiously keeping
Watch over the cash
Liquid eyes peeping
As cool raindrops splash.

Principal subject
His diligent dog
The artist collects
Without dialogue.

Pauline A Wicks

WINTER WARMTH

Together we ambled,
We walked hand in hand
By sparkling reservoirs splitting the land
Calm waters lap closely, a road runs between
Drakes weave through the ripples, necks ruffled in green.
Bright sunlight reflected, its wintry heat
Awakens the cold earth trampled by feet.
Trees show their skeletons, stark in the sun
Grateful for winter's compassionate run.
Jagged and greedy they grab for the light
Soon to be shrouded disguised from our sight
A day like no other so fragile, so rare
Together we ambled, we hadn't a care.
The air it was tranquil in pure atmosphere
And trickling streams with their waters so clear
Converged on the lake, now replenished and full
From storm clouds quite recent on days that were dull.
Today quite a contrast, we ambled together.
We wondered at nature, inspired by the weather.

Wendy Brennan

My Garden

I sit alongside the elderberry tree
Admiring the bluebells standing so proudly

Their blue heads bobbing lightly in the breeze
Full of pollen, just waiting for the bees

The forget-me-nots, a mass of tiny blue
Remind me of the day, when I said 'I do'

The cherry blossom is as white and soft as snow
Soon the bright red cherries will begin to grow

The daffodils and tulips are now past their best
Going back into the ground for a long earned rest

Primula and primrose adding colour here and there
Pansies with their smiling faces are everywhere

The broom is bursting with a golden yellow glow
The peony with its deep crimson is a splendid show

Everything is late this year, nature wanted it that way
But it's May 24th and my garden, well, what a display.

Carol Deakin

ESCAPING

I can't be seen to those who love me,
To those who can, I'm just a figure -
A figure wading in the cool clear water,
A figure touching the glistening sand.
The houses seem smaller and almost lifeless,
The people are mechanical dolls and somewhat unreal.
I turn my back to the world, and all that's in it.
Only facing the peaceful, contrasting horizon.
I feel free and focused,
I'm not being judged nor misinterpreted
I'm at one with nature.

Deborah Carol Hughes

On Leaving Ilfracombe One Sunday In June '78 - Church Bells

As I walked up the hill
One sunny, Sunday morn,
The sun was glistening on the harbour and sea
Painting a beautiful picture
In my memory
Then, I heard the peal of church bells and I felt reborn
I know not why I feel this way
Whenever church bells ring
I think perhaps, for me they bring
The peace on earth when Christmas comes
The joy, as a bride
The peace we felt when war was over
We rang them then with pride
I guess I'll always feel this way
Whenever church bells ring
They stir my heart, and remind me of
So many lovely thing
English valleys, country lanes
Weddings, christenings,
Sweet voices singing
Peace to all, on that lovely Sunday morn
In Devon's lovely Ilfracombe
That sunny, Sunday morn in June.

Irene G Corbett

Clouds

Ribbons of pure white frothy clouds,
Shade the moon, and stars like shrouds,
Moon glowing through, against the dark night
Peeks out between, with shafts of light,
Changing constantly, to glimpse in between,
The brightest star I've ever seen.

How calm it seems, as I watch them pass,
Like wisps of candyfloss,
Floating, gently drifting past,
For words, I'm at a loss.

They don't obscure my vision,
As I watch them late this night,
Peering through my window,
In awe, of clouds in flight.
Such a beautiful sight, I sigh,
For me, this night.

Sheila Duguid

TIMELESS

We drove my love and I, leaving the streets of London behind us,
In the early hours, speeding south, the traffic growing less with each mile travelled.
Even though it was high summer, the time was right for the journey,
The excitement and intensity as we sat in his Healey 3000, racing through the darkness,
Impatient to reach our destination and commence our first holiday together.
Well past the midnight hour we reached Andover and onto Amesbury,
We hit Somerset some hours later, stopping for gas and a quick coffee.
There was a chill in the air, but the glow we felt inside from the anticipation,
Was more than enough to keep even the darkest thought at bay.

The warmth of the car cosied our outstretched legs,
The low leather seats contouring our bodies perfectly,
Devon was soon beneath our wheels, Crediton and Okehampton flashed by,
More refreshments required at the next service station.
Launceston appeared and we drove at a slower pace now,
A fine mist began to tease the headlights,
The A30, a long and windy road reduced our speed even more.
It was nearing 4am when we came upon Bodmin Moor.
Surrounded by an even thicker mist, we slowed and pulled off the road,
We stepped from the car and stood together.
Alone for a second, until we heard the gentle sound of the ponies nibbling grass;
We watched them amble slowly across the deserted road, illuminated in cars' lights,
The mist hiding their hooves, they seemed to be walking on air, almost phantom-like.
It was beautiful, magical to see.

We continued to stand ensconced in each other's arms,
Simply listening to the silence, smelling the cold crisp air,
It was as if we had been transported in time, to another world, another dimension,

Surrounded by this mysterious peace, we watched the dawn break.
The mist dissolving in the morning sun, the ponies walking away to
their secret haunts;
My love and I, stayed for a while, wondering at the aura
of this timeless place,
Neither of us ever wanting to leave, or break the spell.

Amanda-Lea Manning

Thankfully

No more a sound like raging bulls
Snorting red-hot steam
No more the blinkered monsters
Or the shrill of whistle's scream

No more the smell of boiler's smoke
When near bursting at the seam
No more the double headers
Both pulling as a team.

No more an age of spotting
For a moving sight to see
No more the hours of waiting
Or a spotter's cry of glee.

No more the sight of liveries
Of reds and browns and creams
No more the age of footplates
Destroyed this boy's dreams.

No more maybe
But thankfully
Theres Severn Valley Steam.

T Stevenson

Gloucestershire Harvest

Just after 9am, the little ways
For horse and cart are journeys to a time
Still near us; under vaulting leaf and twig
Each lane will covet shadow like a brook;
At clovered margins, rabbits pause to drink.
To cross now is to paddle in the shade,
Those flickers round your ankles, passing cold
Like ripples full of newts or lively elvers,
As fluid as a stir disturbing bees
Intruding thumb-deep in the foxglove bells,
All stumbling dusty raiders of the nectar,
And hornets on bruised fruit in hedgerow trees.

Rare wraiths of herb and other perfumes find us;
The white crinoline blooms of the privet
Scented like dowagers; honeysuckle,
The brandy smell of lilies floating wide.
No quiet in the meadow, where grasshoppers
Rub patience on the heat, then start again.
Now tractors start up - grumbling at the slopes
In neighbour-fields: the shouts and songs of men.
The hay must be in haystacks by the night;
Our heads are full of larks; the sun is loud
And golden flames are scattering through rye,
From terrier breezes, coursing down the light.

Gary Bills

PAST-PRESENT

I am not the truth,
Nor am I a lie.
I am the depravity;
Clothed in the blanket snow of innocence:
The choking memories
Of debauchery past.

I breathe,
The air of collective death
A testament to all;
A deviant conscience of genocide.

The home of silent screams,
Where a nation's feelings echo unfelt
Against crumbling walls of abject agony.
Where fear still slithers between the grey walls:
The unmarked graves of the many unknown
Victims of the yesterdays that cannot be forgot.

The voices of obliteration's,
Nation, cry
How?
Why?
Whose were the faces?
Where were their places?
Annihilation of races.
Where is the love?

Nicolette E Jones

AN ENCHANTED ISLAND

A beautiful island, unique in Greece
Where here you will find an abundance of peace
Its virgin beauty declares it to be
The most picturesque in the Ionian Sea

The bold rugged mountains conflict with the calm
Of the crystal clear sea and its placid charm
Sailing boats glide in a leisurely way
While ferry boats chug to a schedule each day

The attraction of the village can boast
Traditional architecture - the envy of most
The picturesque harbour - the captivating views
The fish taverners for a meal or two

The whitewashed houses: narrow cobbled streets
Without their flowers would not be complete
Profuse Bougainvillaea cascades every wall
Creating an artistry beyond recall

The sheep roam the gorse with their bells ringing clear
While the donkey's bray tells his journey is near
His load is a burden, but onward he'll trudge
With time of no essence, despite the odd nudge

Here we remember the times that have gone
And the peaceful life people try to prolong
With its own character their ways are set
Since tourism has left no 'evidence' yet!

And why should we aim to alter an isle
With such beauty and such a unique style?
Why change a culture existing for years
And bring to this haven a time fraught with fears?

G M Neary

But On An Impulse

Not recently, not after careful thought,
    but on an impulse, in day's early pride,
    wheeling on my bicycle (too awed to ride)
    Spring bright on every side,
I entered Hampton Court.

Not recently; sad years between so bleak
    with war and waste and godlessness and greed.
    But memory that, steadfast, does not heed
    matters that interplead,
holds that prized morning, vivid and unique.

Three scores of years have gone upon their way
    since that May garden, dew-jewelled, washed with rain;
    those palace courts. I have gone there again
    seeking, always in vain,
the unsought magic of that magic day.

It's not some morning's outing that has grown
    in memory to play so prime a part,
    perpetual partner of a wondering heart,
    wondering at the art
that made me, passing, through, made me alone

(none else was there) a witness of the vast
    pageant of prelates, princes, queens and kings,
    statesmen, advisors on world-warping things,
    scholars whose ponderings
gave Holy Writ an English voice at last.

For I was one that day with those whose feet
    - urgent, reluctant, with delight, in fear -
    trod, day by day, year by demanding year
    my morning path.
                So here
    dim past and one that's far more distant, meet.

Martin Summers

The Beach

As I walk along the seashore
With the sea breeze spraying in my face
I know it may not be paradise
But to me it's a special place.
With squashed chips on the pavement
And salt on my lips
A melting ice-cream
That slowly starts to drip.
The sound of the seagulls
Flying overhead
And whispers in the wind
Of things I should have said.
It's a place where I am alone
Yet surrounded by a crowd
A place that I escape to
A place where my conscience I have found.

Lisa Horner

At Sails Point

(Near Bradwell-on-Sea Nuclear Power Station)

Joyful, I stand in Essex, Essex bred,
Sharing this lonely marshscape with St Cedd.

Rimmed by sea-wall, here, like a bowl of corn,
Lie fields that yielded wheat ere Christ was born;
When their rich crop a source of wealth had been
For Cunobelin, Shakespeare's Cymbeline.

See, inland stretch the open fertile leas,
Where drainage dikes stir in the rising breeze,
And swaying rushes, rustling, seem to sing
Soft psalms o'er saltings. Curlews answering.

A strip of silted sand provides a beach:
Here families, bucket-armed, spread out, and reach
To where the tide, foam-frilled, now gently flows,
And lengthening lace-designs lap little toes.

Nearby, a wedge of stone thumbprints the sky:
An ancient chapel beckons passers-by.
Here monks from Lindisfarne were bidden, 'Bring
Your Christian faith, and teach a Saxon king.'

So, thirteen hundred years ago, and more,
St Cedd built here, where Counts of the Saxon shore
Had left a fort to moulder and decay.
Cedd used their bricks: we see them still today.

For he used fabric that was left around.
Even today clear traces on the ground
Show us the line of Roman bank and fosse,
And how Church straddles wall, to form a cross.

This chapel on the wall now looks forsaken;
Yet, come within, see, services still taken!
Where hallowed Saxon stones stride Roman might
The masters of the atom seek for light.

L C Hawke

The Harebell

Hang low the clouds o'er this green land
Where once the skylark rose.
Together we would hand in hand,
Romancing this unbridled land,
Find love where no-one knows.

Hang low the clouds o'er this green land,
Where once the harebell tolled.
Together we would step by step,
Stride islands, countries, lands not met,
To grasp, yet not to hold.

Hang low the clouds o'er this green land
Where once our peace we made.
Our love was earth and wind and sky,
Your arms so strong which let me fly
A memory to fade.

Hang low the clouds o'er this green land
Where once we were so young.
Together we would hold the light
That darkened red into the night.
Be still. That song is sung.

Hang low the clouds o'er this green land
Where once the skylark rose.
Like dandelions our love is blown
To separate pastures yet unknown.
Alone, the harebell tolls.

Maureen Cropley

INFORMATION

We hope you have enjoyed reading this book - and that you will continue to enjoy it in the coming years.

If you like reading and writing poetry drop us a line, or give us a call, and we'll send you a free information pack.

Write to :-

Poetry Now Information
1-2 Wainman Road
Woodston
Peterborough
PE2 7BU
(01733) 230746